Introduction:

Recovering from alcohol and drug addiction is a challenging journey, but with the help of your faith in Christ, it becomes a path of hope, healing, and transformation. This guide provides 100 practical steps to aid you in your recovery process, incorporating spiritual principles and practices that can strengthen your relationship with Christ as you overcome addiction. Remember, recovery is a personal and unique journey, so adapt these steps to your specific needs and consult with professionals when necessary.

We have provided additional space at the bottom of each page for you to create a "plan of action". May God bless you in your journey to Recovery Through Christ!

Acknowledge the Problem

Admit to yourself and to God that you have an addiction and desire to change. Acknowledging a problem with alcoholism or addiction is a crucial and courageous step towards personal growth and recovery. It requires a deep level of self-awareness, honesty, and a willingness to confront the challenges that come with addiction. This book aims to provide insights into how one can acknowledge their struggle with alcoholism or addiction, paving the way for a journey of healing and transformation. Acknowledgment begins with recognizing the signs and symptoms of alcoholism or addiction. Take an honest and introspective look at your relationship with alcohol or substances. Observe patterns of excessive consumption, an increasing tolerance, failed attempts to quit or cut down, neglecting responsibilities or relationships, and experiencing withdrawal symptoms when abstaining.

Plan of action:

_____
_____
_____
_____
_____
_____

Seek Support

Reach out to your church community, pastor, or Christian support groups for guidance, encouragement, and accountability. Recognize and accept that you need help and support in your recovery journey. It's a sign of strength to ask for assistance when facing difficult situations. Consider the people in your life who can provide support—family members, friends, mentors, or support groups. Reach out to them and let them know about your situation and your desire for recovery. Consult with healthcare professionals, such as doctors, therapists, counselors, or addiction specialists, depending on the nature of your recovery needs. They can provide guidance, treatment options, and therapy to support your recovery process. Support groups can be immensely helpful as they provide a safe space to connect with others who have experienced similar challenges. Look for local or online support groups specific to your recovery goals, such as Alcoholics Anonymous, Narcotics Anonymous, or other specialized groups.

Plan of action:

_____
_____
_____
_____
_____
_____

Develop a Personal Relationship With Christ

Engage in daily prayer, Bible study, and meditation to strengthen your spiritual connection. Start with the New Testament, which focuses on Jesus' life, teachings, death, and resurrection. You can also study commentaries, devotionals, and books about Christian faith to deepen your understanding. Regularly reflect on your actions, thoughts, and attitudes. Seek to align them with the teachings of Jesus. Confess your shortcomings and ask for forgiveness when necessary. Develop an intimate and personal connection with Jesus by spending time alone in prayer and contemplation. Share your thoughts, hopes, and fears with Him, and seek His guidance in all aspects of your life. Remember, building a personal relationship with Jesus is a lifelong journey, and it may involve ups and downs. Stay committed, be patient, and allow your relationship with Him to grow organically over time.

Plan of action:

_____
_____
_____
_____
_____
_____
_____

Surrender to God's Will

Submit your addiction and your life to God, trusting in His power to guide your recovery. Build a foundation of trust in God's character and His love for you. Reflect on His faithfulness in the past, and remind yourself of His promises in the Bible. Trust that God's plans for your life are good, even if they may differ from your own. Engage in heartfelt prayer, expressing your desires, concerns, and plans to God. However, also pray for His will to be done above your own. Surrender your own agenda and surrender control of your life to God, inviting Him to lead and guide you. Regularly seek God's guidance through prayer, meditation, and reading the Bible. Pay attention to His voice and the promptings of the Holy Spirit. Seek wisdom from godly mentors or spiritual leaders who can offer guidance and support. Look for signs of God's presence and activity in your life and the world around you. Be attentive to the ways in which He may be directing or shaping your circumstances. Cultivate a posture of openness to His leading.

Plan of action:

_____
_____
_____
_____
_____
_____
_____

Connect With Christian Recovery Programs

Start by researching Christian recovery programs in your area or online. Look for programs that align with your specific needs, such as addiction recovery, mental health support, or other areas of personal struggle. Reach out to local churches, pastors, or Christian counselors and ask for recommendations. They may be familiar with reputable Christian recovery programs in your community. Utilize online resources to find Christian recovery programs. Websites, forums, and social media platforms often provide information about various Christian-based recovery initiatives. Join relevant online communities or groups to connect with others who have similar experiences. Remember, each Christian recovery program may have its own approach and emphasis, so it's essential to find one that aligns with your beliefs, needs, and goals. Building a network of support within the Christian community can provide you with the encouragement and guidance you need on your journey to healing and recovery. Find a Christian counselor or therapist: Seek professional guidance from someone who understands both addiction and the spiritual aspect of recovery.

Plan of action:

_____
_____
_____
_____
_____
_____
_____

Build a Support Network

Surround yourself with fellow Christians who support your recovery journey and can offer understanding and encouragement. Start by reaching out to family, friends, colleagues, or acquaintances who you feel comfortable with and trust. Share your needs or concerns with them and ask for their support. Nurture these existing relationships by being open, attentive, and supportive in return. Participate actively and engage with others who share similar interests, creating opportunities for connection and support. Explore online platforms, forums, or social media groups that focus on topics of interest or support communities. Engage with others in these spaces, sharing your experiences and seeking advice or encouragement. Building a support network requires vulnerability. Be willing to share your struggles, dreams, and aspirations with others. By being authentic, you allow others to connect with you on a deeper level and foster meaningful relationships. Remember, building a support network takes time and effort. Be patient, consistent, and open to new connections. Prioritize quality over quantity, seeking relationships that are genuine, supportive, and uplifting.

Plan of action:

_____
_____
_____
_____
_____
_____

Practice Forgiveness

Practicing forgiveness can be a transformative and healing process. Recognize and honor your feelings of hurt, anger, or betrayal. Allow yourself to fully experience and process these emotions. It's essential to acknowledge and validate your pain before moving towards forgiveness. Reflect on how holding onto resentment or refusing to forgive affects your well-being. Recognize that forgiveness is not condoning the actions or excusing the behavior but freeing yourself from the burden of carrying negative emotions. Try to gain a broader perspective by considering the factors that may have influenced the person's actions. Recognize their humanity and the possibility of them making mistakes or acting out of their own pain. Cultivate empathy by trying to understand the other person's point of view. Consider their circumstances, struggles, or limitations that may have contributed to their actions. Extend compassion towards them, acknowledging that they, too, are flawed human beings. Remind yourself that forgiveness is an act of self-care and liberation, allowing you to move forward and heal. Remember, forgiveness is a personal journey, and the timeline and process will vary for each individual. Be patient and kind to yourself as you navigate this process of letting go and healing.

Plan of action:

_____
_____
_____
_____
_____
_____
_____

Release Resentment and Bitterness

Let go of the resentment, bitterness, and desire for revenge that may be weighing you down. Release these negative emotions by journaling, talking to a trusted friend, or seeking professional support. Find healthy ways to express and process your emotions. Reflect on the reasons behind your resentment and bitterness. Explore the events, actions, or words that led to these emotions. Understanding the root causes can help you gain perspective and clarity. Find healthy outlets to express and release your emotions. Write in a journal, engage in physical activity, or talk to a trusted friend or therapist. Expressing your feelings can provide catharsis and create space for healing. Direct your energy towards positive aspects of your life. Engage in activities that bring you joy, pursue hobbies, or focus on personal goals. Shifting your attention away from the source of resentment can help diminish its hold on you. Remember, releasing resentment and bitterness is a journey that requires patience, self-reflection, and intentional effort. Be gentle with yourself and celebrate each step forward on the path towards healing and forgiveness.

Plan of action:

_____
_____
_____
_____
_____
_____

Set Boundaries

Forgiveness does not mean forgetting or allowing further harm. Establish healthy boundaries to protect yourself from future harm and ensure your emotional well-being. Take time to understand your needs, values, and limits. Reflect on what feels comfortable and uncomfortable for you in different areas of your life, such as relationships, work, and personal space. Determine the specific boundaries you want to establish. These can include emotional boundaries, physical boundaries, time boundaries, or communication boundaries. Clearly and assertively communicate your boundaries to others. Use "I" statements to express how you feel and what you need. Be direct, respectful, and specific about the behavior or action that violates your boundaries. Consistency is key in enforcing boundaries. Stick to your boundaries and follow through with the consequences you have communicated. This helps establish a sense of trust and respect for your boundaries. Remember, saying no to others is saying yes to yourself. Remember, setting boundaries is an ongoing process. It requires consistent communication, self-awareness, and self-advocacy. By setting and maintaining healthy boundaries, you create a space for healthy relationships and personal well-being.

Plan of action:

_____
_____
_____
_____
_____
_____

Practice Self-Compassion:

Be gentle with yourself throughout the forgiveness process. Recognize that healing takes time and that you may experience setbacks or moments of anger or sadness. Acknowledge your pain, struggles, and challenges. Be aware of the emotions and thoughts that arise during difficult times. Self-compassion starts with understanding that suffering is a part of the human experience. Offer yourself the same kindness and support you would offer to a friend in need. Avoid self-criticism, self-judgment, and harsh self-talk. Recognize and challenge any negative or self-critical beliefs you hold about yourself. Replace them with more compassionate and realistic thoughts. Remind yourself that everyone makes mistakes and experiences setbacks, and that it's an opportunity for growth. There are various self-compassion exercises you can try, such as writing self-compassionate letters, visualizations, or guided meditations specifically designed to cultivate self-compassion. These exercises can help you develop a more compassionate mindset. Remember that self-compassion is a skill that takes time and practice to develop. Be patient with yourself and approach the process with a sense of kindness and curiosity.

Plan of action:

_____
_____
_____
_____
_____
_____
_____

Seek Support

Seeking support for drug and alcohol addictions is an important step towards recovery. Schedule an appointment with a healthcare professional, such as a doctor, counselor, therapist, or addiction specialist. They can assess your situation, provide guidance, and recommend appropriate treatment options. Educate yourself about the available treatment options for drug and alcohol addiction. This may include inpatient or outpatient rehabilitation programs, counseling, support groups, or medication-assisted treatment. Individual therapy or counseling sessions can provide a safe and confidential space to address the underlying causes and triggers of your addiction. A therapist or counselor can help you develop coping strategies, set goals, and work through emotional issues related to your addiction. If your addiction is severe or you require a structured environment, consider residential or outpatient rehabilitation programs. These programs provide a comprehensive approach to recovery, including detoxification, therapy, counseling, education, and aftercare planning. Remember, seeking support is a sign of strength and courage. You don't have to face addiction alone, and there are resources and people available to help you on your path to recovery.

Plan of action:

_____
_____
_____
_____
_____
_____

Attend Church Regularly

Participate in worship services, join small groups, and engage in fellowship to stay connected to the body of Christ. Church provides a space for believers to come together and worship God collectively. It offers an opportunity to express gratitude, praise, and adoration through prayers, songs, and rituals. Churches often offer opportunities for spiritual growth through sermons, teachings, Bible study groups, and educational programs. Regular attendance provides access to these resources, which can help Christians deepen their understanding of Scripture and grow in their faith. Attending church regularly allows Christians to connect with their religious traditions, rituals, and the heritage of their faith. It can provide a sense of continuity with the historical roots of Christianity and a connection to the broader body of believers throughout time. It's important to note that while attending church can be beneficial for many Christians, it is not the sole measure of one's faith or spirituality. Personal relationships with God, individual study of Scripture, and a commitment to living out one's faith in daily life are equally important.

Plan of action:

_____
_____
_____
_____
_____
_____
_____

Embrace Accountability

Find an accountability partner who can help you stay on track and provide support during difficult times. Define your goals and objectives clearly. Ensure they are specific, measurable, achievable, relevant, and time-bound (SMART goals). Having clear goals provides a clear direction for your actions and helps you stay focused. Communicate your goals with trusted individuals, such as friends, family, or mentors. Sharing your goals creates a sense of external accountability as others become aware of your intentions. They can provide support, encouragement, and help hold you accountable. Regularly assess your progress towards your goals. Keep track of your achievements, challenges, and any deviations from your plan. Use tools like a journal, calendar, or task management system to record and review your progress. When you make a mistake or fall short of your commitments, take ownership of it. Admitting your mistakes and taking responsibility is a crucial aspect of accountability. Remember, practicing accountability is an ongoing process that requires self-discipline, self-reflection, and a commitment to personal growth. It is a skill that can be developed over time, and the more you practice it, the more it becomes a natural part of your life.

Plan of action:

_____
_____
_____
_____
_____
_____

Practice Self-Care

Prioritize your physical, emotional, and spiritual well-being through exercise, healthy eating, adequate sleep, and relaxation techniques. Ensure you get enough sleep to support your overall well-being. Establish a consistent sleep routine, create a sleep-friendly environment, and aim for 7-9 hours of quality sleep each night. Participate in physical activities that you enjoy. Whether it's going for a walk, practicing yoga, hitting the gym, or playing a sport, regular exercise can boost your mood, reduce stress, and improve your overall health. Nourish your body with balanced and nutritious meals. Include a variety of fruits, vegetables, whole grains, lean proteins, and healthy fats in your diet. Stay hydrated by drinking an adequate amount of water throughout the day. Engage in activities that bring you joy and relaxation. Dedicate time to hobbies, such as painting, reading, playing a musical instrument, gardening, or any other activity that sparks your interest and allows you to unwind. Take breaks from excessive screen time and unplug from digital devices. Engage in activities that do not involve technology, such as going for a nature walk, practicing mindfulness, or reading a book. Listen to your body and take regular breaks throughout the day.

Plan of action:

_____

_____

_____

_____

_____

_____

Replace Unhealthy Habits

Start by recognizing and understanding the specific unhealthy habit you want to replace. Be clear about what triggers the habit, when it occurs, and the negative effects it has on your life. Establish clear and specific goals for replacing the unhealthy habit. Make sure the goals are achievable and realistic within your current circumstances. Break down the goals into smaller, manageable steps to track your progress. Identify healthier alternatives that can fulfill the same needs or provide similar benefits as the unhealthy habit. For example, if you're trying to quit smoking, you might replace it with chewing sugar-free gum, engaging in physical activity, or practicing deep breathing exercises to manage cravings. Modify your environment to support your new habits. Remove triggers or cues that are associated with the unhealthy habit and replace them with cues that remind you of the healthier behavior. Surround yourself with supportive people who encourage and reinforce your positive changes. Remember that replacing unhealthy habits is a gradual process. Be kind to yourself, and don't get discouraged if progress is slow. Focus on the positive changes you're making and the overall improvement in your well-being.

Plan of action:

_____
_____
_____
_____
_____
_____

Memorize Scripture

Commit key Bible verses to memory to draw strength and encouragement during moments of temptation or weakness. Before memorizing a particular verse, take the time to understand its meaning within the broader context of the passage or chapter. This will help you grasp the verse's significance and aid in its memorization. Begin by reading the verse or passage aloud several times to familiarize yourself with the words and structure. Then, repeat it multiple times, gradually reducing your reliance on the written text. Divide the verse into smaller sections or phrases and memorize them individually. Focus on memorizing one section at a time and then gradually combine them until you can recite the entire verse accurately. Regularly review previously memorized verses to reinforce your memory. Repetition is crucial for long-term retention, so make it a habit to revisit the verses you have already learned. Remember, the goal of memorizing scripture is not just to recite words but to internalize and apply the teachings in your daily life. Combine memorization with reflection and understanding to deepen your spiritual growth.

Plan of action:

_____
_____
_____
_____
_____
_____

Practice Gratitude

Develop a habit of expressing gratitude to God for His blessings and for the progress you are making in your recovery. Set aside a few minutes each day to write down things you are grateful for. It can be as simple as three things or moments that brought you joy or appreciation. Reflect on the positive aspects of your life, both big and small. Start your day by expressing gratitude for the things you often take for granted. Before getting out of bed, think about the blessings in your life, such as your loved ones, your health, the opportunities you have, or the simple pleasures that bring you joy. Engage in mindfulness exercises or meditation that focus on gratitude. During these practices, bring your attention to the present moment and intentionally reflect on the things you are grateful for. This can help shift your mindset and bring awareness to the positive aspects of your life. Acts of kindness and service to others can generate a sense of gratitude. Look for opportunities to help someone in need, volunteer your time, or contribute to causes that are meaningful to you. The act of giving can foster gratitude within yourself. Remember, gratitude is a habit that requires practice and consistency. Over time, as you consciously cultivate gratitude, you may notice an increased sense of happiness, contentment, and overall well-being in your life.

Plan of action:

_____
_____
_____
_____
_____
_____

Attend Christian Retreats

Seek opportunities to deepen your faith, gain new insights, and connect with others on a similar journey. Look for Christian retreats that align with your interests and spiritual goals. You can search online, ask your local church or community, or check with Christian organizations for retreat opportunities. Consider factors such as location, theme, duration, and the type of retreat. Make sure the retreat fits your preferences and availability. Prior to attending the retreat, spend some time preparing yourself spiritually. Engage in prayer, meditation, and reflection to cultivate a receptive and open mindset. Consider setting specific intentions or goals for the retreat to guide your experience. While at the retreat, immerse yourself fully in the experience. Participate in the scheduled activities, such as worship, teaching sessions, small group discussions, and prayer times. Be open to connecting with fellow retreat attendees, sharing your thoughts and experiences, and listening to others. Attending a Christian retreat can be a transformative experience, providing an opportunity to deepen your faith, build community, and gain fresh perspectives. Embrace the retreat with an open heart and a willingness to grow, and trust that God will meet you in that space.

Plan of action:

_____
_____
_____
_____
_____
_____
_____

Stay Away From Triggering Environments

Avoid places, people, or situations that may tempt you to relapse, especially in the early stages of recovery. Reflect on past experiences to identify common patterns or themes that are triggering. Once you have identified your triggers, establish clear boundaries to protect yourself. Communicate your limits to others, whether it's expressing your needs or stating what you are comfortable with or not comfortable with. Setting boundaries helps create a sense of safety and control over your environment. If you anticipate being in a potentially triggering environment, develop a plan to manage it effectively. This might include identifying a support person who can accompany you, practicing relaxation techniques or coping strategies, or having a predetermined exit strategy if you feel overwhelmed. If you find that triggering environments significantly impact your well-being and daily functioning, consider seeking support from a mental health professional. They can provide guidance, coping strategies, and therapeutic interventions tailored to your specific needs. Remember, avoiding triggering environments entirely may not always be possible or practical. In such cases, developing effective coping mechanisms and support systems becomes essential.

Plan of action:

_____
_____
_____
_____
_____
_____

Foster Healthy Relationships

Surround yourself with supportive, positive, and spiritually grounded individuals who encourage your growth and sobriety. Establish open and honest communication as the foundation of your relationship. Practice active listening, express your thoughts and feelings clearly, and be receptive to the perspectives of others. Effective communication fosters understanding, resolves conflicts, and builds trust. Treat others with respect and kindness, valuing their opinions, boundaries, and autonomy. Respectful relationships involve honoring each other's individuality, being considerate of each other's needs, and avoiding demeaning or belittling behaviors. Trust is the cornerstone of healthy relationships. Build trust by being reliable, honest, and keeping your commitments. Avoid betraying confidences or engaging in deceitful behaviors. Trust takes time to develop, but it is crucial for building strong and meaningful connections. Dedicate quality time to nurture your relationships. Be present and attentive when spending time with loved ones, creating an environment of connection and shared experiences. Prioritize quality interactions over quantity. Remember that healthy relationships require ongoing effort, patience, and understanding. They evolve over time, and it's important to adapt and grow together. By nurturing healthy dynamics and practicing these principles, you can cultivate strong, fulfilling relationships that enrich your life.

Plan of action:

_____
_____
_____
_____
_____

Find Purpose and Service

Discover your God-given talents and passions, and use them to serve others, both within and outside the church. Spend time in prayer, seeking guidance from God to reveal His purpose for your life. Reflect on your passions, talents, and values, and ask God to guide you in aligning them with His will. Identify the activities, causes, or issues that ignite passion within you. Consider the skills, talents, and resources you possess that can be used to make a positive impact. Reflect on how these passions and gifts can be aligned with the principles and teachings of Christianity. Pay attention to the needs of those around you, both within your immediate circles and in the broader community. Listen to their stories, challenges, and aspirations. This empathetic approach can help you discern how you can best serve and support others. Adopt a humble and servant mindset. Shift your focus from personal gain to serving and uplifting others. Be willing to put the needs of others before your own, seeking opportunities to serve selflessly and without expecting anything in return. Remember, finding purpose and engaging in service is a personal and ongoing process. Be patient with yourself and allow God to guide you as you seek to serve others. Trust that your willingness to serve, even in small ways, can make a meaningful difference in the lives of those around you and bring glory to God.

Plan of action:

_____
_____
_____
_____
_____

Practice Mindfulness

Cultivate a habit of being present in the moment and quieting your mind to listen to God's guidance. Select a passage from the Bible that resonates with you. Read it slowly and attentively, allowing the words to sink in deeply. Reflect on the meaning and how it relates to your life. Pay attention to the emotions and insights that arise as you meditate on God's Word. Practice mindfulness by cultivating gratitude for God's blessings in your life. Take a few moments each day to reflect on the gifts, experiences, and relationships that you are grateful for. Offer prayers of thanksgiving, expressing your appreciation to God for His goodness. Use your breath as an anchor to the present moment. Pay attention to each breath, the rise and fall of your chest or the sensation of air entering and leaving your nostrils. Whenever your mind starts to wander, gently bring your focus back to your breath and the presence of God. Set aside a few minutes each day for self-reflection. Examine your thoughts, emotions, and experiences, inviting God into your inner world. Notice any areas of tension, stress, or unresolved emotions, and surrender them to God in prayer. Remember, mindfulness is a way of deepening your relationship with God and experiencing His presence in the present moment. As you engage in mindfulness practices, invite the Holy Spirit to guide and illuminate your journey, and allow His presence to fill your heart and mind.

Plan of action:

_____
_____
_____
_____
_____
_____

Reflect On God's Love

Reflecting on God's love is a beautiful and transformative practice that can deepen your understanding and experience of His unconditional love for you. Choose Bible verses that emphasize God's love and meditate on them. Read them slowly and repeatedly, allowing the words to sink into your heart and mind. Some verses to consider are John 3:16, Romans 8:38-39, Ephesians 3:17-19, and 1 John 4:9-11. Reflect on the depth, breadth, and sacrificial nature of God's love as revealed in these passages. Recall moments in your life when you have experienced God's love firsthand. Reflect on times when you felt His presence, guidance, comfort, or provision. Consider answered prayers, moments of forgiveness, or instances where you tangibly experienced His love through the actions of others. Take time to express gratitude to God for His love. Verbalize your thankfulness for His unconditional love, for choosing to love you despite your flaws and failures. Express your appreciation for the blessings and benefits that flow from His love. Remember that God's love extends to you personally. Reflect on how God sees you and loves you, embracing your worth and value in His eyes. Extend the same love and compassion to yourself that God offers you. Engage in conversations with other believers about God's love. Share your reflections, experiences, and insights, and listen to how others have encountered God's love in their lives.

Plan of action:

_____
_____
_____
_____
_____
_____

Develop Healthy Coping Mechanisms

Learn healthy ways to manage stress, such as through prayer, deep breathing, or seeking counsel from wise mentors. Develop a personal relationship with God through prayer, meditation, and reading the Bible. Draw strength and comfort from His presence and seek His guidance in difficult times. Invite the Holy Spirit to be your source of peace and wisdom as you navigate challenges. Turn to prayer as a primary means of seeking solace, comfort, and guidance from God. Share your burdens, concerns, and struggles with Him, knowing that He is a loving and compassionate Father who hears and answers prayers. Develop a habit of praying regularly and intentionally. Surround yourself with fellow believers who can provide encouragement, support, and accountability. Engage in a local church or small group where you can share your struggles and experiences, receive prayer and guidance, and offer support to others. Let Christian values and virtues guide your coping mechanisms. Embrace qualities such as forgiveness, humility, patience, and love in your interactions with others. Allow these principles to shape your responses to adversity and help you maintain healthy relationships. Developing healthy coping mechanisms is an ongoing process. It takes time, self-reflection, and a reliance on God's strength and guidance. Be patient with yourself, extend grace, and seek to grow in your faith as you navigate life's challenges with healthy and Christ-centered coping mechanisms.

Plan of action:

_____
_____
_____
_____
_____
_____

Make Amends

Seek to repair relationships damaged by your addiction, making restitution where possible and demonstrating changed behavior. Recognize the harm or wrong you have done and take full responsibility for your actions. Acknowledging your mistakes is the first step towards making amends. Begin by seeking forgiveness from God through prayer. Confess your wrongdoing, express genuine remorse, and ask for His forgiveness. Believe in His grace and trust in His ability to forgive and restore. If possible and appropriate, reach out to the person you have wronged. Choose a suitable time and place to have an open and honest conversation. Express your sincere apologies, acknowledging the specific harm caused, and take ownership of your actions. Avoid making excuses or shifting blame. Use this opportunity for personal growth and learning. Reflect on the lessons you have gained from the experience and commit to making positive changes in your behavior and character. Seek God's guidance in transforming your heart and aligning your actions with His teachings. As you make amends, strive to live a changed life. Allow the experience to shape your character and behavior. Seek to demonstrate integrity, love, and compassion in all your interactions, honoring the teachings of Christ.

Plan of action:

_____
_____
_____
_____
_____
_____

Avoid Isolation

Stay connected with your support network and actively engage in social activities that promote fellowship and mutual support. Make an effort to regularly communicate with others. Reach out to friends, family, or acquaintances through phone calls, text messages, or video chats. Initiate conversations, ask about their well-being, and share your own thoughts and experiences. Showing genuine interest in others fosters meaningful connections. Be open to invitations to social gatherings, parties, or events. Accepting these invitations and actively participating allows you to connect with others and engage in meaningful interactions. Step out of your comfort zone and embrace opportunities for socializing. If you find yourself consistently feeling isolated or struggling to engage with others, consider seeking professional help from a therapist or counselor. They can provide guidance and support in navigating social relationships and overcoming barriers to connection. Overcoming isolation takes effort and intentionality. Be proactive in seeking opportunities for connection, and be patient with the process. By nurturing relationships, engaging in community, and taking care of yourself, you can avoid isolation and cultivate a sense of belonging and connection with others.

Plan of action:

_____
_____
_____
_____
_____

Keep a Journal

Write down your thoughts, emotions, and reflections throughout your recovery journey, capturing both the challenges and the victories. Allocate regular, uninterrupted time for journaling. Find a quiet and comfortable space where you can focus and reflect without distractions. It could be in the morning, before bed, or at any time that works best for you. Before you start journaling, begin with a short prayer, inviting the Holy Spirit to guide your thoughts and reflections. Ask God to speak to you through your journaling and to reveal insights, wisdom, and understanding. Begin your journal entry by expressing gratitude to God. Reflect on the blessings, provisions, answered prayers, and moments of grace you have experienced. Write down specific things you are grateful for and how they have impacted your life. Document instances where you have witnessed God's faithfulness and the answers to prayers. Write down the prayers you have made, and when you see them being answered, note the date, details, and how God has moved in your life. Close your journaling sessions with prayer. Thank God for the opportunity to journal and ask Him to bring reflection, insight, and understanding to what you have written. Pray for continued guidance and growth on your spiritual journey.

Plan of action:

_____
_____
_____
_____
_____

Practice Self-Forgiveness

In Christianity, self-forgiveness is rooted in the belief that God is a loving and forgiving God who offers redemption and grace to all who seek it. While forgiveness is often associated with seeking forgiveness from others or from God, self-forgiveness is an important aspect of the Christian faith because it acknowledges the reality of human imperfection and the need for personal healing and reconciliation. Continually remind yourself of God's grace and His willingness to forgive, allowing yourself to heal from shame and guilt. Recognize and acknowledge the wrongdoing or mistake that requires forgiveness. Confess it honestly before God, acknowledging your responsibility and expressing genuine remorse. Understand that dwelling in guilt and shame can hinder your spiritual growth and prevent you from experiencing the fullness of God's forgiveness. Instead, focus on the transformative power of God's grace and allow it to free you from the burden of guilt. Engage in regular prayer, reading and meditating on Scripture, and participating in a faith community. Allow God's Word to renew your mind and transform your heart, shaping your attitudes and behaviors. Trust in God's love and mercy, and seek guidance from your faith community or spiritual leaders if you need support along the way.

Plan of action:

_____
_____
_____
_____
_____
_____

Participate in Worship and Praise

Participating in worship and praise is an integral part of the Christian faith and can be a deeply enriching experience. Regularly attending church services provides a structured setting for worship and praise. Joining with fellow believers in singing hymns, listening to sermons, and participating in communal prayers can create a sense of unity and connection with God and the community. Prayer is a direct form of communication with God. During worship services or in your personal devotional time, spend time in prayer, expressing your gratitude, confessing your sins, seeking guidance, and offering intercession for others. Take time to reflect on your spiritual journey and experiences of God's faithfulness. Consider keeping a journal where you can write prayers, thoughts, and reflections on your encounters with God. This practice can deepen your awareness of His presence and help you grow spiritually. Worship is not limited to a specific time or place. It extends to how you live your life and treat others. Engage in acts of service, kindness, and love, both within your faith community and in your daily interactions with others. Demonstrating Christ's love through your actions is a form of worship.

Plan of action:

_____
_____
_____
_____
_____
_____

Read Christian Books on Recovery

Reading Christian books on addiction and recovery can be a valuable resource for gaining insights, finding encouragement, and developing a deeper understanding of how faith intersects with the process of overcoming addiction. Look for books specifically focused on addiction and recovery from a Christian perspective. There are various types of books available, including personal testimonies, practical guides, theological reflections, and Bible-based studies. Research online, seek recommendations from trusted sources, or consult with your pastor or a Christian counselor to find suitable titles. Establish a regular reading schedule to ensure consistency. Allocate specific times during the day when you can devote uninterrupted focus to reading. Consistency will help you absorb the material and allow for reflection and application. Before diving into your reading, take a few moments to pray and ask God to guide your understanding and provide clarity. As you encounter challenging concepts or personal reflections, pause to meditate and seek God's wisdom and guidance. As you read, look for practical applications of the concepts and principles discussed in the books. Consider how you can integrate the insights into your own recovery journey and daily life. Be open to making changes and adopting new strategies or habits that align with your Christian faith and contribute to your healing and growth.

Plan of action:

_____
_____
_____
_____
_____
_____

Attend Addiction Recovery Support Groups

Attending addiction recovery support groups as a Christian can be a valuable and supportive step in your journey towards healing and overcoming addiction. Look for addiction recovery support groups that have a Christian focus or incorporate Christian principles into their program. Examples of such groups include Celebrate Recovery, Christian 12-Step programs, or faith-based counseling services. Search online, ask your pastor or church community for recommendations, or reach out to local Christian organizations for information. Once you've identified a Christian-based support group, reach out to them to gather more information. Contact the group leaders or organizers to inquire about meeting times, locations, and any specific requirements for attending. They can provide you with details about the group's structure, format, and what to expect. Make a commitment to attend support group meetings consistently. Regular attendance allows you to build relationships, gain support, and benefit from the group's resources and insights. Participate actively in discussions, share your experiences, and be open to receiving feedback and encouragement from others. Engage in conversations and build relationships with fellow group members. Share your struggles, victories, and prayer requests, and listen empathetically to others. Cultivate a sense of community and support within the group, fostering an environment where individuals can uplift and encourage one another.

Plan of action:

_____
_____
_____
_____

Develop a Daily Routine

Developing a daily routine as a Christian can provide structure, deepen your relationship with God, and help you grow spiritually. Start your day by setting aside dedicated time for prayer, Bible reading, and meditation. This intentional time of communion with God sets the tone for the rest of your day. You can choose a specific time in the morning or find a time that works best for you. Incorporate regular Bible reading into your daily routine. Choose a reading plan or devotional book that suits your interests and goals. Reflect on the passages you read, journal your thoughts, and seek to apply the teachings to your life. Engage in activities that nurture your spiritual growth. This may include listening to Christian podcasts or sermons, reading Christian books, participating in small group Bible studies, or attending church services. Incorporate these activities into your daily routine to deepen your understanding of faith and God's Word. Look for opportunities to serve and show Christ's love to others. Acts of kindness and service can be integrated into your daily routine, whether it's volunteering, reaching out to someone in need, or offering a listening ear. By serving others, you embody the teachings of Jesus and grow in your faith. While having a routine is beneficial, it's also important to remain flexible and adaptable. Life can be unpredictable, and circumstances may require adjustments to your routine. Embrace the need for flexibility while still prioritizing your spiritual practices.

Plan of action:

_____
_____
_____
_____

Identify and Address Underlying Issues

Identifying and addressing underlying issues is an important part of personal growth and healing as a Christian. Take time for self-reflection and introspection. Ask God to reveal any underlying issues or areas of brokenness in your life. Pray for wisdom, discernment, and the courage to confront and address these issues. Engage in honest self-examination, allowing yourself to explore your thoughts, emotions, and behaviors. Journaling can be a helpful tool in this process, as it allows you to express your feelings, identify patterns, and gain clarity about underlying issues. Addressing underlying issues often requires vulnerability and transparency. Be willing to admit your struggles, weaknesses, and areas of brokenness to God, yourself, and others whom you trust. Recognize that you are not alone in your struggles and that seeking help and support is a sign of strength, not weakness. Once you've identified underlying issues, develop a plan of action to address them. This might involve seeking therapy, engaging in personal development resources, attending support groups, or making changes in your habits and relationships. Be intentional and consistent in implementing these steps. Surround yourself with a supportive Christian community that can offer love, encouragement, and accountability. Engage in fellowship, small groups, or church activities where you can receive support and prayer.

Plan of action:

_____
_____
_____
_____
_____

Renew Your Mind

Renewing your mind as a Christian is a transformative process of aligning your thoughts, beliefs, and perspectives with God's truth. Regularly read and study the Bible to gain a deeper understanding of God's truth. Meditate on Scripture, reflect on its meaning, and apply it to your life. Make it a habit to incorporate Bible reading into your daily routine, allowing God's Word to shape your thoughts. Prayer is a powerful tool in renewing your mind. Spend time in prayer, not only making requests but also seeking God's guidance, wisdom, and transformation. Ask Him to renew your mind and help you align your thoughts with His truth. Pay attention to your thought patterns and identify any negative or ungodly beliefs that may be hindering your spiritual growth. Whenever negative or untrue thoughts arise, challenge them with God's truth found in Scripture. Replace them with thoughts that are in line with God's Word and His promises. Be mindful of what you allow into your mind. Avoid exposure to media, entertainment, or conversations that promote ungodly thinking or values. Fill your mind with uplifting and edifying content that aligns with God's truth. Invite the Holy Spirit to guide and transform your mind. Surrender to His leading and allow Him to work in you, empowering you to think and respond in ways that are pleasing to God.

Plan of action:

_____
_____
_____
_____

Practice Perseverance

Practicing perseverance as a Christian involves maintaining steadfastness, endurance, and faithfulness in the face of challenges, setbacks, and trials. Reflect on the lives of biblical figures such as Abraham, Joseph, Moses, and Paul, who endured hardships and remained faithful to God. Let their stories inspire and encourage you. Prayer is a powerful source of strength and guidance. Regularly communicate with God, seeking His wisdom, strength, and encouragement. Pour out your heart, express your struggles, and ask for His help to persevere through difficult times. Recognize that the Christian journey is a marathon, not a sprint. Keep your focus on the eternal and trust in God's faithfulness. Remember that God is working all things together for your good and His glory, even if you face temporary trials or setbacks. Invite the Holy Spirit to empower and guide you in your perseverance. Trust in His strength and guidance as you navigate challenges and difficulties. Surrender to His leading and rely on His power to sustain you. Above all, trust in the faithfulness of God. Remind yourself of His promises and remember that He is with you every step of the way. Lean on His strength, knowing that He will provide the endurance and perseverance you need to overcome any obstacle.

Plan of action:

_____
_____
_____
_____
_____

Create a Relapse Prevention Plan

Creating a relapse prevention plan as a Christian involves incorporating faith-based principles and practices into your strategies for maintaining sobriety and overcoming temptations. Begin by seeking God's guidance through prayer. Surrender your struggles, weaknesses, and desires to Him, acknowledging your need for His strength and help in maintaining sobriety. Trust in His power to transform your life. Take time to identify the triggers and high-risk situations that may lead to relapse. These can include certain people, places, emotions, or activities that have been associated with your addictive behaviors in the past. Prioritize self-care activities that promote your overall well-being. This includes getting enough rest, eating a healthy diet, engaging in regular exercise, and pursuing activities that bring you joy and fulfillment. Taking care of yourself physically, mentally, and emotionally helps reduce stress and supports your recovery journey. Set healthy boundaries in your relationships and activities to safeguard your recovery. This may involve distancing yourself from people or situations that may trigger or enable your addictive behaviors. Communicate your boundaries clearly and seek support in maintaining them. Regularly review and evaluate your relapse prevention plan. Stay accountable to your support network and be honest about your struggles and victories. Celebrate milestones and make adjustments as needed to address new challenges or triggers that arise.

Plan of action:

_____
_____
_____
_____
_____

Seek Forgiveness From Those You've Harmed

Seeking forgiveness from others as a Christian involves acknowledging your wrongdoing, taking responsibility for your actions, and actively seeking reconciliation and restoration. Take time to honestly reflect on your actions and recognize the harm or hurt you may have caused. Acknowledge your mistakes and the impact they had on others. Begin by praying to God for guidance, humility, and a sincere desire to seek forgiveness. Ask the Holy Spirit to reveal any blind spots or areas where you need to make amends. Initiate a face-to-face or, if necessary, a heartfelt written conversation with the person you have wronged. Choose an appropriate setting where you can have a private and honest conversation. Clearly and sincerely express your remorse for your actions and any pain or harm you caused. Take full responsibility for your behavior without making excuses or blaming others. Offer a sincere apology without reservation. Use "I" statements to convey your understanding of the impact of your actions, such as "I am sorry for...," "I regret...," and "I understand how my actions affected you." Allow the person to share their feelings, thoughts, and experiences related to the situation. Be attentive, compassionate, and willing to listen without becoming defensive. Show empathy and seek to understand their perspective. Ask the person how you can make things right or how you can actively work towards healing and reconciliation. Be open to their suggestions and willing to take appropriate actions to rectify the situation.

Plan of action:

_____
_____
_____
_____

Explore Christian Music

Exploring Christian music can be a wonderful way to connect with God, express your faith, and find inspiration. Christian music encompasses a wide range of genres, including contemporary, worship, gospel, hymns, rock, hip-hop, and more. Consider your personal taste in music and the genres that resonate with you. This will help you narrow down your search and find Christian artists within those genres. Explore Christian music through streaming platforms such as Spotify, Apple Music, or YouTube Music. These platforms often have curated playlists, genre categories, or Christian music charts that can help you discover new artists and songs. Additionally, websites and blogs dedicated to Christian music can provide insights, reviews, and recommendations. Explore their discography and see which songs resonate with you. Look for Christian music concerts or festivals happening in your area. These events can expose you to a variety of Christian artists and allow you to experience the music in a live setting. It's a great opportunity to discover new artists and immerse yourself in the worship experience. As you listen to Christian music, pay attention to the lyrics and messages conveyed in the songs. Reflect on the biblical truths, spiritual encouragement, and themes of faith, hope, and love that are present. Allow the lyrics to deepen your connection with God and inspire you in your Christian journey.

Plan of action:

_____
_____
_____
_____
_____

Engage in Physical Activities

Getting engaged in physical activities is a great way to improve your overall health and well-being. Determine what you want to achieve through physical activities. Whether it's improving your fitness level, losing weight, building strength, or simply staying active, setting clear goals will give you a sense of purpose and motivation. Find physical activities that you genuinely enjoy. This could be anything from walking, jogging, swimming, cycling, dancing, hiking, playing a sport, or joining a fitness class. When you enjoy what you're doing, it becomes easier to stay consistent and committed. Keep things interesting and prevent boredom by incorporating a variety of activities into your routine. Mix up cardio exercises, strength training, flexibility exercises, and activities that challenge different muscle groups. This variety not only keeps you engaged but also helps promote overall fitness and prevent overuse injuries. Schedule your physical activities as you would any other important appointment or commitment. Set specific days and times for your workouts, and treat them as non-negotiable. Consistency is key when it comes to reaping the benefits of physical activity. Find ways to make physical activities enjoyable and something you look forward to. Listen to music, podcasts, or audiobooks while you exercise, or explore beautiful outdoor locations for your activities. Create an environment that enhances your enjoyment and makes it a pleasant experience.

Plan of action:

_____
_____
_____
_____
_____

Practice Self-Reflection

Practicing self-reflection is an excellent way to gain self-awareness, understand your thoughts and emotions, and make meaningful changes in your life. Find a peaceful environment where you can focus without distractions. This could be a cozy corner in your home, a park, or any place where you feel at ease. Allocate a specific time for self-reflection, whether it's daily, weekly, or monthly. Consistency is key to developing a reflective habit. Reflect on your core values, principles, and beliefs. Consider whether your actions align with your values and whether any adjustments are needed. Reflect on recent events, interactions, or situations that had a significant impact on you. Consider how you responded, what you learned, and how you can grow from those experiences. Spend time alone without distractions. Disconnect from technology, engage in activities like walking in nature, listening to music, or engaging in hobbies that allow for introspection. Reflect on past mistakes or failures without judgment. Focus on the lessons learned and how you can apply them to future situations. Be kind and gentle with yourself throughout the process. Avoid self-criticism and instead cultivate self-compassion. Treat yourself with understanding, forgiveness, and acceptance. Remember, self-reflection is a lifelong journey. The more you practice, the more self-awareness you'll develop, and the better equipped you'll be to make choices aligned with your values and goals.

Plan of action:

_____

_____

_____

_____

Serve Others In Recovery

One of the most valuable ways to serve others in recovery is by providing emotional support and encouragement. Be a listening ear, offer words of encouragement, and show empathy and understanding to those going through the recovery process. Your personal story of overcoming challenges and finding hope and healing through your faith can inspire and encourage others. Share your testimony with individuals in recovery, support groups, or through platforms where you can reach a wider audience. Foster an environment where individuals in recovery feel safe, accepted, and supported. Offer your home as a meeting place for support groups, or organize fellowship activities that promote healthy social connections and a sense of belonging. Recovery can involve various challenges, such as finding employment, housing, or accessing healthcare services. Offer practical assistance by helping individuals navigate these processes, providing resources, or connecting them with appropriate organizations or support networks. Take the time to educate yourself about addiction, recovery, and the challenges individuals face during the healing process. This knowledge will help you better understand and support those in recovery, and enable you to provide more effective assistance. Approach individuals in recovery with love, compassion, and a non-judgmental attitude. Create an atmosphere where they feel safe and accepted, regardless of their past mistakes or struggles. Treat them as equals, recognizing their inherent dignity and worth.

Plan of action:

_____
_____
_____
_____

Prioritize Sobriety

Prioritizing sobriety involves aligning one's actions, mindset, and lifestyle with biblical principles and the teachings of Jesus Christ. Begin by seeking God's guidance through prayer and studying His Word, the Bible. Ask for strength, wisdom, and the Holy Spirit's help in overcoming temptations and staying committed to sobriety. Recognize that you have a responsibility to take care of your body, which is a temple of the Holy Spirit (1 Corinthians 6:19-20). Accept that sobriety is your personal choice and commit to making decisions that honor God and prioritize your well-being. Identify and avoid environments, situations, or people that may trigger cravings or temptations for substance use. This might involve distancing yourself from old social circles or making changes in your lifestyle to remove sources of temptation. Cultivate self-discipline through the power of the Holy Spirit. Develop healthy habits, such as setting boundaries, managing stress through prayer and meditation, and practicing self-care. Exercise self-control and rely on God's strength to resist temptation. Maintain a close relationship with God through consistent prayer and worship. Seek His guidance, strength, and forgiveness. Engage in regular worship and fellowship with other believers to stay rooted in your faith. Celebrate your milestones and victories along the journey of sobriety. Recognize and acknowledge God's faithfulness in your life and the progress you've made.

Plan of action:

_____
_____
_____
_____

Attend Christian Counseling

Attending Christian counseling can be a beneficial step in seeking emotional and spiritual support. Research and identify Christian counseling services or therapists in your area. You can search online directories, ask for recommendations from your local church or Christian community, or consult with your pastor or spiritual leader. Look for counselors who are licensed professionals with relevant credentials and experience in providing Christian counseling. Consider their approach to therapy, ensuring it aligns with your beliefs and values. Before your first session, think about the challenges, concerns, or goals you want to address in counseling. Consider what specific aspects of your faith or spirituality you would like to integrate into the counseling process. Christian counseling typically incorporates biblical principles, spiritual guidance, and prayer into the therapeutic process. Discuss your desire to integrate your faith into the counseling sessions with your therapist, and work collaboratively to explore how your faith can inform your healing and growth. Build a trusting and supportive relationship with your counselor. Express your needs and preferences, and provide feedback on how the counseling process is working for you. Open communication will help your counselor understand your progress and make adjustments as necessary. Consistency is crucial in counseling. Attend sessions regularly as scheduled and commit to the counseling process.

Plan of action:

_____
_____
_____
_____

Learn to Manage Stress

Develop healthy stress-management techniques, such as deep breathing, prayer, or engaging in relaxing activities. Managing stress involves relying on your faith and integrating biblical principles into your approach. Turn to prayer as a means of connecting with God, expressing your concerns, and seeking His guidance and peace. Pray regularly, both individually and with fellow believers, entrusting your worries to God and asking for His strength and wisdom. Spend time meditating on God's Word. Find verses that speak to your current stressors, such as those related to trust, peace, and casting your burdens on the Lord. Memorize and reflect on these verses to remind yourself of God's promises and the assurance of His presence. Learn to say no when necessary and set healthy boundaries to avoid becoming overwhelmed by excessive commitments. Prioritize your well-being and make time for rest, relaxation, and spiritual nourishment. If stress becomes overwhelming or persistent, do not hesitate to seek professional help from counselors or therapists who can provide guidance and support. Christian counselors who integrate faith into their practice can help you navigate stress from a holistic perspective. Take intentional moments to rest in God's presence, knowing that He is your refuge and strength. Practice stillness, quiet reflection, and allowing yourself to be renewed by His peace. Trust that God will provide the strength and grace you need to navigate stressful situations.

Plan of action:

_____
_____
_____
_____

Build Healthy Boundaries

Building healthy boundaries is an essential aspect of maintaining your well-being and creating healthy relationships. Start by developing a clear understanding of your own needs, values, and limits. Reflect on what makes you feel comfortable or uncomfortable in different situations and interactions. Determine the areas in your life where you need to establish boundaries. This can include emotional, physical, mental, and time boundaries. Consider the situations, people, or behaviors that tend to overstep your limits. Consistency is key to maintaining healthy boundaries. Stick to your boundaries even when it feels challenging or uncomfortable. This helps others understand that your boundaries are important to you. It's okay to say no when something doesn't align with your boundaries or when you don't have the capacity to take on additional responsibilities. Remember that saying no is not selfish; it's an act of self-care and self-respect. If you find it challenging to establish or maintain boundaries, seek support from a trusted friend, family member, or therapist. They can provide guidance, encouragement, and help you navigate through difficult situations. Remember that building healthy boundaries is a process that takes time and practice. Be patient with yourself and give yourself permission to prioritize your well-being.

Plan of action:

_____
_____
_____
_____
_____

Develop a Spiritual Toolkit

Developing a spiritual toolkit as a Christian can help you deepen your faith, grow spiritually, and navigate life's challenges. Cultivate a consistent prayer practice. Set aside time each day to communicate with God, express gratitude, seek guidance, and share your concerns. Prayer helps foster a personal relationship with God and provides a sense of peace and connection. Regularly attend a church or Christian community where you can worship, learn, and fellowship with fellow believers. Participate in communal activities such as worship services, small groups, and service projects. Engaging in worship and fellowship helps nurture your faith and provides opportunities for growth, accountability, and support. Read books, articles, and other resources that enrich your understanding of Christianity, spirituality, and personal growth. Choose materials that align with your beliefs and values, and explore different genres such as theology, Christian classics, biographies, or inspirational writings. Reading can provide fresh perspectives and insights to nourish your spiritual journey. Dedicate time for personal reflection and journaling. Write down your thoughts, prayers, and reflections on your spiritual journey. Journaling helps you process experiences, gain clarity, and document your spiritual growth over time.

Plan of action:

_____
_____
_____
_____
_____

Cultivate a Spirit of Humility

Cultivating a spirit of humility is a valuable virtue that can enhance your character, relationships, and spiritual growth. Acknowledge your strengths and achievements, but also be aware of your limitations and areas for growth. Understand that you are not perfect and that everyone has strengths and weaknesses. Adopt a mindset of continual learning and growth. Be open to new ideas, perspectives, and feedback. Recognize that you don't have all the answers and that there is always more to learn. Seek opportunities to expand your knowledge and skills.
Emphasize the power of prayer: Prioritize prayer as a means to seek God's guidance, strength, and healing throughout your recovery journey. Truly listen to others without interrupting or rushing to express your own thoughts. Seek to understand their perspective and show genuine interest in what they have to say. Avoid assuming that you always know best or dismissing others' opinions without consideration. Seek to understand and empathize with the experiences, struggles, and emotions of others. Treat everyone with kindness, respect, and dignity. Cultivating empathy and compassion helps break down barriers of superiority and fosters a humble and caring attitude. Take care of your physical, mental, and emotional well-being. Engaging in self-care activities helps maintain a balanced perspective and prevents burnout. It also allows you to better care for others with a genuine and humble heart.

Plan of action:

_____
_____
_____
_____
_____

Reflect On the Consequences of Addiction

Find a quiet and comfortable environment where you can reflect without distractions. Allow yourself to be honest and open about the consequences of your addiction. Take time to acknowledge and accept the negative consequences your addiction has had on various aspects of your life. This may include relationships, physical health, mental well-being, career or education, financial stability, and personal fulfillment. Allow yourself to feel the emotions that arise as you reflect on the consequences of addiction. It may bring up feelings of guilt, shame, regret, sadness, or anger. Recognize that these emotions are a natural part of the healing process. Reach out to a trusted friend, family member, or a professional counselor who can provide support and guidance during your reflection process. Sharing your thoughts and emotions with someone you trust can help alleviate the burden and provide a fresh perspective. While it's important to acknowledge the negative consequences, also consider the positive aspects that can arise from your reflection. Recognize that reflecting on the consequences of addiction is a crucial step towards making positive changes in your life and breaking free from the grip of addiction. Let the reflection on the consequences of addiction serve as a source of motivation to make positive changes in your life. Use it as a reminder of why you want to overcome addiction and the potential benefits that lie ahead.

Plan of action:

_____
_____
_____
_____
_____

Foster Healthy Friendships

Fostering healthy Christian friendships can provide support, accountability, and spiritual growth. Look for people who share your Christian values and beliefs. Attend church activities, join small groups or Bible studies, and participate in Christian organizations or volunteer opportunities. Surrounding yourself with like-minded individuals creates a foundation for meaningful friendships. Be yourself and allow others to be authentic as well. Share your thoughts, struggles, and joys openly with your friends. Authenticity fosters trust and creates an environment where deeper connections can develop. Truly listen to your friends, seeking to understand their joys, challenges, and spiritual journeys. Show empathy and offer support when they face difficulties. Practice active listening by giving them your full attention and validating their feelings and experiences. Cultivate an atmosphere of mutual accountability where you can help each other grow spiritually. This can involve checking in regularly, discussing challenges, and holding each other accountable to Christian values and behaviors. Encourage one another to pursue righteousness and offer gentle correction when needed. Recognize that friendships take time to develop and deepen. Lift your friendships up in prayer. Ask God to guide and bless your relationships, to help you be a good friend, and to bring like-minded individuals into your life. Prayer can strengthen your friendships and invite God's presence into your relationships.

Plan of action:

_____
_____
_____
_____
_____

Avoid Overconfidence

Avoiding overconfidence involves cultivating humility and recognizing the importance of relying on God's guidance rather than solely relying on your own abilities. Recognize that all your talents, skills, and accomplishments come from God. Understand that everything you have is a gift from Him, and humbly acknowledge that you are not self-sufficient. Embrace a mindset of gratitude for God's blessings. Cultivate a habit of prayer and regularly seek God's guidance and wisdom. Pray for humility and self-awareness, asking God to reveal any areas of overconfidence in your life. Remember that prayer is a way of acknowledging our dependence on God. Engage in acts of service and humility. Look for opportunities to help others, recognizing that true greatness is found in serving others rather than seeking personal glory. By focusing on the needs of others, you can develop a humble and compassionate attitude. Develop a habit of expressing gratitude to God for His blessings and acknowledging His role in your life. Praise Him for His faithfulness and provision, which helps to keep your heart focused on God's greatness rather than your own achievements. When you face failures or setbacks, view them as opportunities for growth and learning. Recognize that you are not infallible and that mistakes happen. Use these experiences as humbling moments to seek God's guidance, learn from your errors, and improve.

Plan of action:

_____
_____
_____
_____

Create a Gratitude List

Creating a gratitude list is a wonderful practice that can help you focus on the positive aspects of your life and cultivate a grateful heart. Find a quiet and comfortable space where you can reflect without distractions. Set aside a specific time, such as the beginning or end of the day, to create your gratitude list. Begin your gratitude list by acknowledging the simple and essential things you often take for granted. These can include having a roof over your head, access to clean water, food to eat, good health, or the love and support of family and friends. Acknowledge both the ordinary and extraordinary aspects of your life. Appreciate the small daily joys and the extraordinary moments that have brought you happiness or growth. Consider challenges or difficult times you have faced and the lessons you have learned from them. Express gratitude for the personal growth, resilience, or insights gained through those experiences. Make it a habit to review your gratitude list regularly. You can revisit it daily, weekly, or whenever you need a reminder of the blessings in your life. This practice will help you maintain a grateful mindset. Consider sharing your gratitude list with others or expressing your appreciation directly to the people or things you are grateful for. This can deepen your connections with others and inspire gratitude in their lives as well.

Plan of action:

_____
_____
_____
_____
_____

Celebrate Milestones

Celebrating sobriety milestones as a Christian is an opportunity to give glory to God for His transformative work in your life. Begin by expressing heartfelt gratitude to God for His grace, strength, and guidance throughout your journey of sobriety. Pray, thanking Him for His faithfulness, healing, and deliverance from addiction. Take time to reflect on your journey of recovery. Consider the challenges you have overcome, the progress you have made, and the ways in which your faith has played a role in your sobriety. Reflect on the lessons learned and the personal growth you have experienced. Your sobriety milestone can be an opportunity to share your testimony with others, both within your faith community and beyond. Share how God has transformed your life, how your faith has given you strength, and how surrendering to Him has helped you overcome addiction. Your story can be an encouragement and inspiration to others who may be struggling. Consider seeking guidance from your pastor, a Christian counselor, or a mentor who can provide spiritual insight and support. They can help you navigate the emotions, challenges, and spiritual aspects of your journey. Reaffirm your commitment to sobriety and to God. Dedicate yourself to continued growth, accountability, and reliance on His strength. This milestone is not an endpoint but a reminder to remain steadfast in your faith and sobriety.

Plan of action:

_____
_____
_____
_____
_____

Develop Spiritual Disciplines

Spiritual disciplines are practices that help you engage with God, draw closer to Him, and conform your life to His will. Regular prayer is vital in developing a deeper connection with God. Set aside specific times to pray, both individually and communally. Pray for guidance, thanksgiving, confession, and intercession. Engage in regular study of the Bible to understand God's word and apply it to your life. Choose a reading plan, study a specific book or topic, and reflect on the message and teachings of Scripture. Periodically fast from food or other activities to focus your attention on God, seek His guidance, and cultivate self-discipline. Fasting can be a powerful tool for spiritual growth and surrendering your desires to God. Serve others as an expression of your faith. Look for opportunities to love and help those in need, both within the church community and in the wider world. Serving others is a tangible way to live out your faith and imitate Christ. Regularly examine your thoughts, motives, and actions in light of God's truth. Confess any sins or areas where you fall short, seek forgiveness, and strive for repentance and growth. Set aside regular times for rest and rejuvenation, both physically and spiritually. Use this time to disconnect from the busyness of life, reflect on God's goodness, and recharge your spiritual batteries. Developing spiritual disciplines is a journey, and it requires consistency and perseverance. Start with small steps and gradually incorporate these practices into your daily life.

Plan of action:

_____
_____
_____
_____
_____

Find Solace In Nature

Finding solace in nature can be a beautiful way for Christians to connect with God's creation and experience His presence. Spend time in quiet contemplation while surrounded by nature. Find a peaceful spot outdoors, whether it's a park, garden, forest, or any natural setting, and intentionally observe and appreciate the beauty of God's creation. Reflect on the intricate details, the interplay of colors and textures, and the harmony of the natural world. Engage in prayer and worship while in nature. Use the serene environment as an opportunity to lift up your praises, thanksgiving, and petitions to God. Find a secluded spot where you can express your heart to Him, whether it's through spoken words, songs, or simply being still and listening to the sounds of nature. Take regular walks or hikes in natural surroundings. Engage your senses by paying attention to the sights, sounds, smells, and textures around you. As you immerse yourself in nature, let it be a time of communion with God, where you seek His presence, listen for His voice, and find solace in His creation. Use nature as inspiration for artistic expression. Paint landscapes, write poetry, compose music, or engage in any creative endeavor that allows you to capture the beauty of God's creation. Through the creative process, you can further connect with God and express your gratitude and awe for His handiwork. Consider attending Christian retreats or visiting retreat centers located in natural settings.

Plan of action:

_____
_____
_____
_____
_____

Scripture-based Affirmation

Practicing scripture-based affirmation involves using the truths and promises found in the Bible to affirm and declare positive statements about yourself and your life. Choose Bible verses that speak to the specific areas of your life or aspects of your character that you want to affirm. Look for verses that offer encouragement, assurance, guidance, or reminders of God's promises. You can use a concordance or search online for relevant verses. Take time to meditate on the selected scriptures. Read them slowly, multiple times, and allow their meaning to sink in. Reflect on the implications of these verses for your life and your relationship with God. Craft affirmations based on the chosen scriptures that are personal and applicable to your situation. Rewrite the verses in the first person and present tense, transforming them into positive statements that affirm who you are and what you believe. For example, if the verse says, "I can do all things through Christ who strengthens me" (Philippians 4:13), the affirmation can be, "I am capable of overcoming any challenge through the strength of Christ within me." Practice the affirmations consistently. Repeat them daily, multiple times if possible, to reinforce the positive declarations in your mind and spirit. Repetition helps to reprogram negative thought patterns and replace them with biblical truths. Carry the affirmations with you throughout the day. Write them down on index cards or use a note-taking app on your phone. Refer to them whenever you need encouragement or a reminder of God's truth. Use them as a guide to shape your thoughts, decisions, and interactions with others.

Plan of action:

_____
_____
_____
_____

Practice Discernment

Practicing discernment as a Christian involves seeking wisdom from God to make sound judgments and decisions in accordance with His will. Begin by seeking God's guidance through prayer. Approach Him with humility, acknowledging your need for wisdom and understanding. Ask the Holy Spirit to lead and enlighten you, to grant you discernment in every situation you face. Immerse yourself in the Word of God. Regularly study and meditate on Scripture to familiarize yourself with God's principles, teachings, and character. The Bible provides a solid foundation for discernment, as it reveals God's truth and helps you recognize His voice. Cultivate a sensitive ear to the Holy Spirit's promptings and guidance. The Holy Spirit is the ultimate source of wisdom and discernment. Pay attention to His still, small voice speaking to your heart and guiding you in the right direction. Be patient and willing to wait for God's timing when making important decisions. Rushing into choices without seeking His guidance can lead to poor outcomes. Trust that God knows what is best for you and that His timing is perfect. Recognize that discernment is a lifelong process, and mistakes may occur along the way. Embrace them as opportunities for growth and learning. When you make wrong choices, humbly seek God's forgiveness, course-correct, and allow Him to teach and mold you through the experience.

Plan of action:

_____
_____

Share Your Testimony

Sharing your testimony as a Christian is a powerful way to proclaim the work of God in your life and testify to His transforming grace. Take time to reflect on your journey of faith and the specific ways God has worked in your life. Consider the key moments, experiences, or encounters with God that have impacted you. Identify the main themes, such as your life before Christ, how you encountered Christ, and the transformation and growth you've experienced since then. Organize your thoughts and experiences into a coherent and concise narrative. Write down the key points and transitions to help you share your testimony in a clear and focused manner. Consider the main message or lesson you want to convey through your story. Make your testimony relatable to the audience you're sharing with. Connect your story to universal themes and struggles that others may face. Highlight the ways in which God's grace, love, or power can impact and transform their lives as well. Include specific details and examples that illustrate the significant moments, encounters, or insights in your journey. These details help listeners grasp the depth and authenticity of your experience with God. Be sensitive to the context and the needs of your audience. Respect the diversity of perspectives and experiences present. Share your story with humility, avoiding judgment or condemnation of others. Let love and compassion guide your words. Pray for opportunities to share your testimony with others, and ask God to guide you in choosing the right moments and circumstances. Seek the leading of the Holy Spirit in discerning when and how to share your story.

Plan of action:

_____
_____
_____

_____

Embrace Vulnerability

Embracing vulnerability as a Christian is about being willing to open your heart and share your authentic self with God and others, trusting in God's love, grace, and strength. Understand that God loves you unconditionally, regardless of your flaws, weaknesses, or past mistakes. Embracing vulnerability begins with knowing that you are fully accepted and cherished by your Heavenly Father. Meditate on passages such as Romans 8:38-39 and John 3:16 to remind yourself of God's unfailing love for you. Seek and cultivate relationships with other Christians where you can be genuine, transparent, and vulnerable. Create spaces where you can share your struggles, doubts, and joys. Create a space where others feel comfortable expressing their thoughts, concerns, and emotions. Practice empathy, understanding, and compassion as you engage with others and seek to understand their perspectives and experiences. Embracing vulnerability may involve seeking healing and restoration from past hurts, wounds, or traumas. Be willing to acknowledge and address areas of brokenness in your life, seeking support through counseling, therapy, or prayer ministry. Allow God to work in those vulnerable places to bring healing and wholeness. Engage in vulnerable and honest conversations with God through prayer. Pour out your heart to Him, expressing your doubts, fears, and deepest desires. Trust that God is a compassionate and understanding Father who welcomes your vulnerability and longs to meet you in your most vulnerable moments.

Plan of action:

_____
_____
_____
_____

Go On a Christian Mission

Begin by praying and seeking guidance from God. Ask for clarity and discernment in understanding how you can best contribute to a Christian mission. Seek His direction in choosing the right mission organization or project that aligns with your values, skills, and passions. Explore different mission organizations that align with your interests and values. Look for organizations that focus on areas or causes that resonate with you, such as humanitarian aid, evangelism, education, healthcare, social justice, or community development. Research their mission, values, and the types of opportunities they offer. Reflect on your skills, talents, and interests. Consider how you can contribute your unique abilities to a mission project. Mission work involves a wide range of tasks, such as teaching, construction, healthcare, administration, counseling, and more. Identify areas where you can make a meaningful impact based on your abilities. Reach out to the mission organizations you have identified and express your interest in volunteering or joining their projects. Inquire about their application process, requirements, and available opportunities. Some organizations offer short-term mission trips, while others have long-term commitments. Choose an option that suits your availability and commitment level. If you engage in international missions, be prepared to learn and respect different cultures, customs, and languages. Educate yourself about the local context and strive to build genuine relationships with the people you serve. Embrace humility, openness, and a willingness to learn from others.

Plan of action:

_____
_____
_____
_____

Seek Christian Mentors

Seeking Christian mentors can greatly benefit your spiritual growth and provide valuable guidance in your faith journey. Begin by praying and asking God to guide you in finding the right Christian mentors. Seek His wisdom and discernment in identifying the individuals who can offer guidance, wisdom, and support. Engage actively in your church community and participate in activities such as small groups, Bible studies, or ministry teams. By doing so, you will have the opportunity to interact with other believers who may serve as mentors or have connections with potential mentors. Pay attention to individuals within your existing relationships who demonstrate maturity, wisdom, and a deep faith in Christ. Consider approaching them and expressing your desire for mentorship, asking if they would be willing to invest in your spiritual growth. Take the initiative to reach out to potential mentors. Express your admiration for their faith, character, or wisdom, and share your desire to learn from them and receive their guidance. Request a meeting or a regular time for mentorship. When connecting with a potential mentor, establish clear expectations and goals for the mentoring relationship. Clear communication and shared understanding will help foster a fruitful mentorship experience. Once you find a mentor, be committed to the relationship. Respect their time, insights, and wisdom. Be punctual, prepared, and engaged during your meetings. Value and appreciate their investment in your spiritual growth.

Plan of action:

_____
_____
_____
_____

Pray For Spiritual Armor

Praying for spiritual armor is a powerful way to seek God's protection and strength against spiritual battles and temptations. The concept of spiritual armor is derived from Ephesians 6:10-18, where the apostle Paul encourages believers to put on the full armor of God. Pray for God's truth to surround and guide you. Ask for discernment and a deep understanding of His Word. Pray that you would be firmly rooted in the truth of Scripture and that lies and deception would be exposed and overcome. Pray for God's peace to guard your steps and guide your interactions with others. Ask for opportunities to share the good news of Jesus Christ and His love. Pray for God's peace to reign in your relationships and for His grace to resolve conflicts and bring reconciliation. Pray for the assurance of your salvation through Jesus Christ. Ask for God's protection over your mind, thoughts, and beliefs. Pray that you would be filled with hope, confidence, and the knowledge of your identity as a child of God. Pray for the ongoing guidance and empowerment of the Holy Spirit as you engage in spiritual warfare. Ask for His leading in prayer, intercession, and spiritual discernment. Pray that you would be sensitive to His promptings and open to His work in your life. Pray for God's protection over every area of your life. Ask for His angels to guard and shield you from the schemes of the enemy. Pray for His divine intervention and deliverance from spiritual attacks or oppression.

Plan of action:

_____
_____
_____
_____

Stay Committed to Therapy

Staying committed to therapy as a Christian involves recognizing the value of seeking professional help, being intentional in your approach, and integrating your faith into the therapeutic process. Practice patience: Recovery takes time, and progress may not always be linear. Trust in God's timing and remain patient with yourself and the process. Understand that therapy is a valuable tool for emotional, mental, and spiritual growth. Recognize that seeking therapy is not a sign of weakness but rather a courageous step towards healing and wholeness. Look for a therapist who is respectful of your Christian beliefs and integrates a faith-based approach into their practice. A therapist who understands and values your faith can help you integrate your spirituality into your therapeutic process. Make therapy a priority by scheduling regular sessions and committing to attending them consistently. Treat therapy as an essential part of your self-care and spiritual growth. Recognize that therapy may involve challenging moments and require you to confront difficult emotions or beliefs. Lean on your Christian community for support and encouragement. Share your therapy journey with trusted friends, mentors, or spiritual leaders who can provide guidance, accountability, and prayer support. Embrace the process of growth and change, trusting that God is working through the therapeutic journey to bring healing and transformation. Actively incorporate your faith into your therapy sessions.

Plan of action:

_____
_____
_____
_____

Engage in Christian Art

Engaging in Christian art can be a meaningful and enriching way to express your faith and connect with God. Christian art encompasses a wide range of forms, including visual arts (painting, drawing, sculpture), music, poetry, literature, dance, and more. Explore various art forms to find the ones that resonate with you and allow you to express your faith creatively. Study the works of renowned Christian artists throughout history. Explore the works of painters like Michelangelo or Rembrandt, or listen to the compositions of classical Christian musicians like Bach or Handel. Allow their artistic expressions to inspire and guide your own creative process. Approach your art as an act of worship and a way to connect with God. Offer your creativity and talents to God, seeking His guidance and inspiration as you create. Cultivate a mindset of surrender and allow your art to become a form of prayer and worship. Attend art exhibitions, concerts, or performances that showcase Christian art. Participate in events that celebrate and explore the intersection of faith and art. Engaging with the work of other Christian artists can inspire and challenge your own artistic endeavors. Embrace a spirit of growth and experimentation in your artistic journey. Be willing to try new techniques, explore different mediums, and step outside your comfort zone. Allow yourself to learn and grow as an artist, trusting that God can work through your creative process.

Plan of action:

_____
_____
_____
_____

Develop a Crisis Plan

Developing a recovery crisis plan as a Christian involves preparing yourself spiritually, emotionally, and practically to navigate difficult times. Begin by seeking God's guidance and wisdom as you develop your recovery crisis plan. Pray for discernment and clarity in understanding the steps you need to take and the resources you may need during a crisis. Reflect on your past experiences and identify the triggers and warning signs that may indicate a crisis situation. These could be emotional, relational, or situational factors that tend to contribute to your struggles or challenges. Understanding these triggers and signs can help you be proactive in addressing potential crises. Outline specific steps and actions to take in the event of a crisis. This may include contacting specific individuals in your support network, reaching out to professional counselors or therapists, attending support group meetings, or utilizing crisis hotlines. Write down important contact information and keep it readily accessible. Cultivate a deep and consistent relationship with God through prayer, reading Scripture, and seeking His guidance. Lean on His strength and wisdom during times of crisis, knowing that He is always with you and ready to provide comfort and guidance. Regularly review and update your recovery crisis plan as needed. As you grow and change, your needs and strategies for recovery may evolve. Ensure that your plan remains relevant and aligned with your current circumstances.

Plan of action:

_____
_____
_____
_____

Renew Your Identity In Christ

Renewing your identity in Christ is a lifelong process that involves aligning your thoughts, beliefs, and actions with the truth of who you are in Christ. Internalize and believe what the Bible says about your identity in Christ. Understand that you are a beloved child of God, forgiven, redeemed, and made new. Recognize that your worth and value come from your relationship with Him, not from external factors or achievements. Identify any negative self-talk or beliefs that contradict your identity in Christ. Challenge those thoughts with the truth of God's Word. Replace lies with the truth of who God says you are. For example, if you struggle with feeling unworthy, remind yourself that in Christ, you are chosen and loved unconditionally. Take intentional steps to renew your mind daily. Fill your mind with God's truth by meditating on Scripture, listening to Christian teachings, reading books that align with biblical principles, and surrounding yourself with positive influences. Ask the Holy Spirit to transform your thinking and align it with God's perspective. Pray for the Holy Spirit to reveal and deepen your understanding of your identity in Christ. Ask Him to help you embrace it fully and live it out in your thoughts, words, and actions. Seek His guidance and empowerment to walk in the truth of who you are as a new creation. Live out your identity in Christ through obedience to God's commands and principles. Seek to align your actions and choices with who He says you are. As you surrender to His will and follow His guidance, you will experience the transformative power of living in your true identity.

Plan of action:

_____
_____
_____
_____

Practice Self-Compassion

Practicing self-compassion involves extending kindness, understanding, and acceptance to yourself, especially in times of difficulty, failure, or self-judgment. Start by cultivating mindfulness, which is the practice of being present and aware of your thoughts, feelings, and experiences without judgment. Notice when you're being self-critical or hard on yourself, and gently redirect your attention to the present moment with kindness. Understand that everyone experiences challenges, setbacks, and imperfections. Recognize that you are not alone in your struggles and that it is a part of the human experience. Remind yourself that it is normal to face difficulties and that you deserve compassion and understanding, just like anyone else. Pay attention to your inner dialogue and challenge self-judgment and negative self-talk. Notice when you're being harsh or critical towards yourself and replace those thoughts with kinder and more compassionate statements. Treat yourself with the same care and empathy you would offer to a friend. Be intentional about treating yourself with kindness and care. Offer yourself words of encouragement, understanding, and support. Practice self-nurturing activities that bring you joy and comfort, such as engaging in hobbies, taking time for self-care, or engaging in activities that recharge and replenish your energy. Let go of the need for perfection and embrace your imperfections. Understand that making mistakes, facing challenges, and falling short of your own expectations is a natural part of being human.

Plan of action:

_____
_____
_____
_____

Seek Deliverance Through Prayer

Seeking deliverance through prayer is a powerful way to invite God's intervention and freedom from spiritual bondage or oppressive circumstances. Acknowledge and identify areas of your life where you desire deliverance. This could include areas of sin, addiction, negative thought patterns, emotional burdens, or any form of spiritual oppression. Approach God with a repentant heart, confessing any sins or areas where you have fallen short. Repentance involves turning away from sinful behaviors and attitudes and seeking God's forgiveness and transformation. Pray for God's protection over yourself, both physically and spiritually. Ask Him to surround you with His angels and to shield you from any spiritual attacks or influences that may hinder your deliverance. Speak and declare God's promises over your life. Find Scriptures that speak specifically to the areas where you need deliverance and proclaim them in faith. Claim the victory and freedom that Christ has already won for you on the cross. Pray fervently for God to break chains, strongholds, and any spiritual bondage in your life. Ask Him to reveal and uproot any hidden or deep-seated issues that may be hindering your deliverance. Invite the Holy Spirit to bring conviction, healing, and transformation. In Jesus' name, bind and rebuke any demonic or oppressive forces that may be at work in your life. Command them to leave and release their hold over you. Remember that your authority comes from Christ, and through Him, you have power over the enemy.

Plan of action:

_____

_____

_____

_____

Explore Christian Podcasts

Exploring Christian podcasts can be a great way to deepen your understanding of the faith, gain spiritual insights, and find encouragement in your Christian journey. Consider the specific topics or areas of the Christian faith that you would like to explore further. This could include Bible study, theology, Christian living, relationships, discipleship, apologetics, or specific ministries. Identifying your interests will help you find podcasts that align with your preferences. Look for reviews and recommendations of Christian podcasts from trusted sources, such as Christian websites, blogs, or social media groups. Pay attention to feedback about the podcast's content, production quality, and hosts to ensure it aligns with your preferences. Once you find a Christian podcast that interests you, subscribe to it on your preferred podcast platform. This allows you to receive new episodes automatically and stay updated with the latest content. Additionally, consider following the podcast's social media accounts or joining any communities or discussion groups associated with the podcast. Take notes, reflect, and apply the insights and teachings you gain from the podcasts to your own life and faith journey. Engage in discussions with others who listen to the same podcasts to deepen your understanding and grow together.

Plan of action:

_____
_____
_____
_____

Attend Christian-Based Recovery Retreats

Attending Christian-based addiction recovery retreats can be a meaningful step towards finding support, healing, and spiritual guidance in your journey to recovery. Look for Christian-based addiction recovery retreats in your area or nearby regions. You can search online, ask local churches or religious organizations, or seek recommendations from individuals who have attended similar retreats. Once you find potential retreats, gather information about their focus, duration, location, cost, and any specific requirements they may have. Pay attention to whether they align with your specific needs and beliefs. Each Christian-based retreat may have its own approach to addiction recovery. Some may incorporate counseling, group therapy, Bible study, prayer, meditation, and worship. Take the time to understand the philosophy and methodology of the retreat to ensure it resonates with your personal beliefs and recovery goals. When the time comes, make sure to follow the instructions provided by the organizers regarding arrival, check-in procedures, and the schedule of activities. Be open to participating fully in the retreat's offerings, engage with fellow attendees, and be willing to explore and share your experiences. After the retreat, it's crucial to maintain the momentum and continue seeking support for your addiction recovery. This may include joining local support groups, connecting with church communities, finding a mentor or counselor, or exploring other recovery resources available to you.

Plan of action:

_____
_____
_____
_____

Trust in God's Strength

Rely on God's power, knowing that through Him, you can overcome any temptation and find the strength to persevere. Trusting in God's strength is a personal and spiritual journey that can deepen your faith and provide comfort and guidance in times of difficulty. Study and reflect upon the scriptures and teachings of your faith tradition. Seek to deepen your understanding of God's character, His promises, and the ways He has demonstrated His strength in the past. This knowledge can serve as a foundation for your trust. Recognize that you have limited control over many aspects of life. Surrender your worries, anxieties, and desires to God, trusting that His plans are greater than your own. Acknowledge that His strength is perfect in your weakness and that He is ultimately in control. Recall moments in your life when you have witnessed God's strength or experienced His faithfulness. Reflect on how He has carried you through challenges, provided for your needs, or granted you strength when you felt weak. Reminding yourself of these instances can help build trust in His power. Trusting in God's strength often involves patience and surrendering to His timing. Understand that His plans may not align with your own expectations or desired timeline. Trust that He knows what is best for you and that His strength will be made evident in His perfect timing. Develop a habit of gratitude by acknowledging and appreciating the blessings and provisions in your life. Gratitude helps shift your focus from worries and doubts to the goodness of God.

Plan of action:

_____
_____
_____
_____

Write a Letter to Your Future Self

Writing a letter to your future self can be a powerful and reflective exercise. It allows you to express your current thoughts, hopes, and aspirations while providing a means of self-reflection when you revisit the letter in the future. Decide when you want to open and read the letter in the future. It could be a year from now, five years, or even longer. Having a specific time frame will give your letter more significance and make it easier to track your personal growth. Choose a peaceful environment where you can focus and reflect without distractions. This will allow you to delve into your thoughts and emotions more effectively. Begin your letter with a warm and personal salutation, addressing your future self. You can use phrases like "Dear Future Me," "To the person I am becoming," or create your own unique greeting. Share your dreams, hopes, and aspirations with your future self. What do you want to achieve? What changes do you want to make in your life? Be specific and descriptive, as this will help you measure your progress when you read the letter later. Reflect on the lessons you have learned and the experiences that have shaped you. Consider the challenges you have overcome, the insights gained, and the personal growth you have achieved. Acknowledge any setbacks or mistakes as valuable learning opportunities. Write words of encouragement and support to your future self. Remind yourself of your strengths, resilience, and the belief that you have in your ability to overcome obstacles. Encourage yourself to stay true to your values and pursue your passions.

Plan of action:

_____

_____

_____

_____

Engage In Acts of Service

Engaging in acts of service as a Christian is an excellent way to live out your faith and demonstrate love, compassion, and kindness towards others. Consider your interests, skills, and talents. Reflect on how you can use these gifts to serve others effectively. Whether it's through teaching, mentoring, offering practical assistance, or using creative abilities, find ways to align your service with your God-given abilities. Connect with your church and inquire about existing service opportunities. Many churches have ministries focused on community outreach, serving the poor and marginalized, youth programs, elderly care, or missions. Volunteer to serve in these ministries or express your willingness to help in any way needed. Research local organizations, nonprofits, and charities that align with your passion for serving others. Contact them to inquire about volunteer opportunities or specific needs they have. This could involve helping at homeless shelters, food banks, hospitals, orphanages, or community centers. Look for opportunities to perform random acts of kindness throughout your day. It could be as simple as holding a door open, offering a kind word, giving a compliment, or helping someone in need. These small acts can make a big difference in brightening someone's day and spreading God's love. Approach acts of service with a selfless heart, without seeking recognition or expecting anything in return. Serve others with humility, love, and a genuine desire to make a positive difference in their lives.

Plan of action:

_____
_____
_____
_____

Create a Vision Board

Take some time to reflect on your values, passions, and what you feel God is calling you to pursue. Consider different areas of your life, such as spiritual growth, relationships, career, health, and personal development. Identify specific goals and desires that are in line with your Christian faith. Collect materials for your vision board, including a large poster board or corkboard, scissors, glue or tape, markers or colored pencils, magazines, printed images, quotes, and Bible verses that resonate with your vision. Cut out images, words, and phrases that capture the essence of your vision and goals. Choose visuals and text that inspire and reflect your Christian values, such as images of nature, Bible verses, symbols of faith, and representations of your desired outcomes. Lay out your cutouts on the poster board or corkboard, experimenting with different placements until you are satisfied with the overall arrangement. Consider grouping related items together or creating sections for different areas of your life. Leave enough space for additional elements or modifications in the future. Use markers or colored pencils to write additional affirmations, quotes, or Bible verses directly on the board. You can also include personal prayers or declarations that align with your vision and goals. Take a moment to step back and reflect on your completed vision board. Pray over each aspect of it, dedicating your goals and desires to God's guidance, blessing, and wisdom. Seek His will and ask for His help in aligning your vision with His plans for your life.

Plan of action:

_____
_____
_____
_____

Practice Forgiveness Toward Others

Practicing forgiveness toward others is a powerful and transformative act that aligns with Christian teachings. Begin by understanding what forgiveness truly means. Forgiveness does not mean condoning or excusing the wrongdoing, nor does it require forgetting what happened. Instead, forgiveness is a conscious choice to release feelings of anger, resentment, and the desire for revenge. Make a deliberate choice to forgive the person who has wronged you. This decision may not happen instantly, especially for deep wounds, but commit yourself to the process of forgiveness. Remember that forgiveness is a journey, and it may require ongoing effort. Try to put yourself in the other person's shoes and seek to understand their perspective. Recognize that everyone is fallible and capable of making mistakes. Consider the factors that may have contributed to their actions or attitudes. Empathy can help soften your heart and foster compassion. Release any grudges or resentments you hold towards the person. Holding onto these negative emotions only continues to harm you. Choose to free yourself from the burden of carrying these feelings, and make a conscious effort to let them go. Forgiveness and reconciliation are separate processes. While forgiveness is a personal choice, reconciliation involves rebuilding trust and restoring the relationship. Depending on the circumstances, reconciliation may or may not be possible or advisable. It's important to consider factors such as safety, boundaries, and the other person's willingness to change.

Plan of action:

_____
_____
_____
_____

Keep a Recovery Journal

Creating a recovery journal can be a helpful tool to support your journey towards healing and growth. Select a journal that appeals to you, whether it's a blank notebook, a guided journal specifically designed for recovery, or an electronic journaling app. Find something that you feel comfortable using and that suits your personal preferences. Clarify the purpose of your recovery journal. Determine what you want to achieve through journaling. It could be self-reflection, tracking progress, expressing emotions, exploring triggers, identifying patterns, setting goals, or celebrating milestones. Having a clear intention will guide your journaling process. Find a quiet and comfortable environment where you can journal without distractions. Consider lighting candles, playing soothing music, or creating a calming atmosphere that helps you relax and focus. Allow your recovery journal to be a space where you can freely express your emotions, both positive and negative. Write about your victories, struggles, fears, frustrations, gratitude, hopes, and dreams. Be honest and authentic in your writing. Use your recovery journal to track and reflect on your progress. Write about the milestones you have achieved, the lessons you have learned, and the growth you have experienced. Celebrate your successes, no matter how small they may seem. Use your recovery journal to set meaningful goals and intentions for your healing journey. Write down specific, achievable goals that align with your recovery and personal growth.

Plan of action:

_____

_____

_____

_____

Seek Opportunities For Praise and Worship

Seeking opportunities for praise and worship as a Christian can enhance your spiritual growth and deepen your relationship with God. Regularly attend your local church's worship services. Participate wholeheartedly in the worship portion of the service, singing praises, praying, and engaging with the worship team and congregation. Church services provide a community of believers coming together to worship God. If you have musical gifts or a passion for singing, consider joining a worship team or choir at your church. This involvement allows you to use your talents to lead others in worship and be part of a dedicated group focused on praising God. Look for Christian concerts, conferences, or events in your area. These events often feature renowned worship leaders and artists who lead powerful times of praise and worship. Attending such events can be inspiring and rejuvenating for your spiritual life. Carve out time in your daily routine for personal worship. Set aside moments of solitude to worship God through prayer, singing, reading the Bible, and meditating on His goodness. Use worship songs, hymns, or instrumental music to help create an atmosphere of praise. Set aside a dedicated space in your home for worship. Decorate it with items that inspire you, such as a Bible, candles, or artwork. Play worship music, sing, and spend time praising God in this sacred space.

Plan of action:

_____
_____
_____
_____

Embrace a spirit of gratitude

Embracing a spirit of gratitude is a transformative mindset that can bring joy, contentment, and a deeper appreciation for life. Take time to reflect on your life and the blessings you have received. Consider the relationships, experiences, opportunities, and material possessions that you are grateful for. Reflect on the positive aspects of your life and the things you often take for granted. Make it a habit to express gratitude every day. Set aside a few minutes each morning or evening to think about or write down a few things you are grateful for. It could be as simple as a beautiful sunrise, a kind word from a friend, a good meal, or a comfortable home. Focusing on the small blessings helps cultivate a grateful heart. Engage in mindful practices that help you stay present and appreciate the current moment. Notice the beauty around you, savor the taste of your food, and embrace the joy in everyday activities. Mindfulness helps you recognize and be grateful for the little moments that often go unnoticed. Train your mind to focus on the positive rather than dwelling on the negative. When faced with challenges or difficulties, consciously choose to look for lessons, growth opportunities, or silver linings in the situation. Shifting your perspective helps you find gratitude even in the midst of adversity. Incorporate gratitude into your prayer life. Take time during your prayers to express thankfulness to God for His love, provision, and blessings in your life. Recognize His faithfulness and goodness, even in challenging times.

Plan of action:

_____
_____
_____
_____

Stay Connected To Scripture

Set aside a specific time each day for reading the Bible. Consistency is key in developing a habit. It could be in the morning, during lunch breaks, or before bed—choose a time that works best for you. Start with a manageable amount of reading, such as a chapter or a few verses, and gradually increase it over time. Select a reading plan that suits your needs and preferences. There are various options available, such as reading the Bible chronologically, following a specific book or theme, or using a devotional guide. Reading plans can provide structure and guidance, helping you explore different parts of the Bible. Utilize study resources such as commentaries, concordances, and study Bibles to deepen your understanding of Scripture. These resources can provide insights into historical context, cultural background, and theological interpretations. Engage in a Bible study group or join a small group at your church. These groups provide opportunities to discuss and delve deeper into Scripture with fellow believers. Sharing insights, asking questions, and hearing different perspectives can enhance your understanding and strengthen your connection to God's Word. Look for opportunities to integrate Scripture into your daily routines and activities. Write down verses on sticky notes and place them around your home or workspace. Use Scripture as the basis for prayers, affirmations, and personal reflection. Let God's Word permeate your thoughts and actions throughout the day.

Plan of action:

_____
_____
_____
_____

Establish Healthy Routines

Establishing healthy routines is a valuable way to prioritize your well-being and create positive habits in your daily life. Determine what areas of your life you want to prioritize and improve. This could include physical health, mental well-being, spiritual growth, relationships, work-life balance, or personal development. Having clarity about your priorities will guide the creation of your healthy routines. Create a schedule or plan that incorporates your goals and priorities. Allocate specific time slots for activities that support your well-being. This might include dedicated time for exercise, meditation, reading, quality time with loved ones, meal planning, or pursuing personal interests. Be intentional about structuring your day to accommodate these routines. Begin by introducing one or two healthy routines at a time. Starting small increases the likelihood of success and prevents overwhelm. As you become comfortable with those routines, gradually add more over time. Small, consistent steps lead to sustainable change. Develop an evening routine that promotes restful sleep and relaxation. Prioritize activities that help you wind down, such as reading, practicing gratitude, reflecting on the day, or engaging in a calming activity. Prepare your environment and mindset for a restful night's sleep. Recognize that life is dynamic, and circumstances may change. Be open to adapting your routines when needed while staying true to your overall goals and priorities.

Plan of action:

_____
_____
_____
_____

Reflect On the Stories of Biblical Figures

Study the stories of individuals in the Bible who faced challenges and found redemption, drawing inspiration and lessons from their experiences. Start by reading the story or passage from the Bible that features the biblical figure you want to reflect on. Read the text carefully, paying attention to the details, context, and the message being conveyed. Gain a deeper understanding of the story by considering the historical and cultural context in which it takes place. Research the background, setting, and circumstances surrounding the biblical figure's life. This can provide valuable insights into the challenges, beliefs, and values of that time. Identify the key themes and messages conveyed in the story. Look for lessons, principles, and truths that can be extracted from the narrative. Consider the challenges, choices, and outcomes experienced by the biblical figure and how they relate to your own life. Reflect on the strengths and weaknesses displayed by the biblical figure. Identify their virtues, character traits, and admirable qualities that you can emulate in your own life. Similarly, recognize any weaknesses, mistakes, or areas for growth that can serve as cautionary lessons. Look for connections between the experiences of the biblical figure and your own life. Consider the challenges, triumphs, and decisions you face and how the lessons from the biblical story can guide and inspire you. Find inspiration in their faith, perseverance, or obedience to God's calling.

Plan of action:

_____
_____
_____
_____

Set Healthy Boundaries With Loved Ones

Clearly communicate your needs, limitations, and triggers to your family and friends, ensuring a supportive environment for your recovery. Take time to identify and understand your own needs, values, and limits. Reflect on what makes you feel comfortable, respected, and emotionally balanced in your relationships. Consider the areas where you may need to set boundaries to protect your well-being. Clearly define the boundaries you want to establish. Be specific about what is acceptable and unacceptable in your relationships. This can include boundaries around personal space, time commitments, emotional support, communication expectations, or any other area that is important to you. t's common for loved ones to react with surprise, resistance, or even pushback when you set boundaries. Stay firm in your decision and remind yourself that setting boundaries is a healthy and necessary practice. Be prepared to kindly and calmly address any objections or attempts to cross your boundaries. Setting boundaries may initially feel uncomfortable or guilt-inducing, especially if you're used to prioritizing others' needs over your own. Remember that setting boundaries is an act of self-care and self-respect. Be kind and patient with yourself as you navigate this process.

Plan of action:

_____
_____
_____
_____

Pursue Spiritual Disciplines

Pursuing spiritual disciplines is an excellent way to deepen your relationship with God, grow in faith, and cultivate spiritual maturity. Start by setting your intention to pursue spiritual disciplines. Recognize the importance of dedicating time and effort to nurture your spiritual life and draw closer to God. Commitment and consistency are key in pursuing spiritual disciplines effectively. Explore and identify the spiritual disciplines that resonate with you and align with your spiritual goals. Some common spiritual disciplines include prayer, meditation, fasting, Bible study, worship, solitude, silence, journaling, serving others, and practicing gratitude. Choose disciplines that you feel drawn to and that will nourish your spiritual growth. Begin with one spiritual discipline at a time to avoid overwhelm and increase your chances of success. Focus on developing a consistent practice before adding additional disciplines to your routine. Once you feel comfortable and consistent with one discipline, you can gradually introduce others. Practice being fully present and attentive during your spiritual disciplines. Minimize distractions by turning off electronic devices, finding moments of solitude, and focusing your thoughts on God. Embrace mindfulness in your prayers, Bible reading, and meditation, seeking to be aware of God's presence in every moment.

Plan of action:

_____
_____
_____
_____

Maintain a Humble Heart

Remain humble in your recovery, acknowledging that your sobriety is a gift from God and staying open to His leading in every step. Acknowledge your strengths and accomplishments, but also be honest about your weaknesses and limitations. Embrace a realistic view of yourself, understanding that you have areas for improvement and growth. Develop the habit of active listening, which involves genuinely listening to others with an open mind and heart. Seek to understand their perspectives, experiences, and wisdom without judgment or defensiveness. Valuing and learning from the input of others is an important aspect of humility. Adopt a learner's mindset by recognizing that there is always more to learn and discover. Approach every situation, interaction, and experience with an attitude of curiosity and openness. Embrace opportunities for growth, be willing to learn from others, and humbly admit when you don't have all the answers. Regularly reflect on your mistakes and shortcomings. Take responsibility for your actions, acknowledge the impact they may have had on others, and seek opportunities for growth and learning. Embrace a mindset of continuous improvement, allowing your mistakes to serve as valuable lessons. Avoid comparing yourself to others, as it can lead to pride or feelings of inadequacy. Embrace your uniqueness and focus on your own journey of growth and development. Celebrate the accomplishments of others without feeling threatened or envious.

Plan of action:

_____
_____
_____
_____

Cultivate a Sense of Purpose

Discover and pursue your unique God-given purpose, aligning your actions and goals with His plan for your life. Take time to reflect on your core values, beliefs, and the things that truly matter to you. Consider the activities, causes, or issues that ignite your passion and bring you joy. Understanding your values and passions is a crucial step in aligning your sense of purpose with what truly matters to you. Explore your unique strengths, talents, and skills. Consider the activities or areas where you excel and find a sense of fulfillment. Recognizing and utilizing your strengths can help you contribute meaningfully to the world and uncover your purpose. Define your short-term and long-term goals. Identify what you want to achieve, experience, or contribute in different areas of your life, such as career, relationships, personal growth, and service to others. Setting clear goals provides direction and helps you focus your efforts toward a purposeful life. Consider the positive impact you want to have on the world around you. Reflect on the ways in which you can use your skills, knowledge, and resources to make a difference. Identify the causes or issues that resonate with you, and explore how you can contribute to them. Remember that cultivating a sense of purpose is a lifelong journey. Be open to new possibilities and allow your purpose to evolve and adapt as you grow and change. Embrace the ups and downs, challenges, and detours along the way, knowing that they are all part of your unique path to purpose.

Plan of action:

_____
_____
_____
_____

Educate Yourself on Addiction

Continually educate yourself about the science, psychology, and effects of addiction, equipping yourself with knowledge to aid in your recovery. Look for workshops, seminars, or conferences related to addiction in your local community or online. These events often feature experts in the field who share their knowledge and insights on addiction. They may cover topics such as the science of addiction, prevention strategies, treatment approaches, and the impact of addiction on individuals and society. Consider volunteering at local addiction treatment centers, support groups, or organizations. This hands-on experience can provide valuable insights and allow you to interact with individuals who are directly impacted by addiction. If possible, explore opportunities to work professionally in the addiction field, such as becoming a counselor, therapist, or advocate. Keep up with the latest research and studies in the field of addiction. Subscribe to reputable journals, newsletters, or online publications that focus on addiction research and advancements in treatment. Staying informed about current trends and scientific findings can enhance your knowledge and understanding of addiction. If you have a specific interest in addiction and want to deepen your understanding, consider seeking professional guidance. Consult with addiction counselors, therapists, or researchers who can provide personalized recommendations, resources, and guidance based on your specific interests and goals.

Plan of action:

_____
_____
_____
_____

Share Your Struggles With Trusted Friends

Reflect on the people in your life whom you consider trustworthy and supportive. These are individuals with whom you feel comfortable sharing your vulnerabilities, knowing that they will maintain confidentiality, offer empathy, and provide non-judgmental support. Consider friends, family members, mentors, or members of your faith community who have demonstrated their care and understanding. Select a suitable time and place to have a private and uninterrupted conversation with your trusted friend. Find a comfortable and quiet setting where you can both focus and engage in meaningful dialogue without distractions. When sharing your struggles, be honest and authentic about what you're going through. Share your emotions, thoughts, and experiences openly, allowing yourself to be vulnerable. Authenticity builds trust and encourages your friend to reciprocate with their own openness and support. After sharing your struggles, listen attentively to your friend's response. Give them space to offer their thoughts, reflections, and support. Acknowledge and appreciate their willingness to listen and provide guidance. Sharing your struggles with trusted friends is often about seeking empathy and validation. Allow your friend to empathize with your experiences, emotions, and challenges. Sometimes, knowing that someone understands and validates your feelings can be incredibly comforting and reassuring.

Plan of action:

_____
_____
_____
_____

Embrace Occasional Solitude

Set aside dedicated time for solitude in your schedule. Choose a time and place where you can be alone without distractions. It could be early mornings, evenings, or weekends when you have fewer commitments and responsibilities. During your solitude time, disconnect from digital devices and social media. Put your phone on silent or in another room to minimize distractions and interruptions. Give yourself permission to detach from the constant influx of information and notifications. Remind yourself of the ways God has been faithful in your recovery journey, strengthening your faith and trust in Him. Use your solitude time to engage in activities that bring you joy and recharge your energy. It could be reading a book, journaling, practicing a hobby, going for a walk in nature, meditating, listening to music, or engaging in creative pursuits. Choose activities that help you connect with yourself and bring a sense of inner peace. Embrace the present moment during your solitude time. Practice mindfulness by paying attention to your senses, observing your thoughts and emotions without judgment, and fully immersing yourself in the present experience. This cultivates a deeper sense of self-awareness and helps you appreciate the beauty and tranquility of solitude. Silence is a powerful aspect of solitude. Embrace silence by spending time in quiet environments, away from noise and distractions.

Plan of action:

_____
_____
_____
_____

Reflect On God's Faithfulness

Find a quiet and comfortable space where you can have uninterrupted time for reflection. Choose a time when you can be fully present and focus on your thoughts and emotions. Engage with Scripture passages that highlight God's faithfulness. Examples include Psalm 136, Lamentations 3:22-23, 2 Timothy 2:13, and Hebrews 10:23. Read and meditate on these passages, allowing them to speak to your heart and reaffirm God's unwavering faithfulness throughout history and in your personal life. As you reflect on God's faithfulness in the past, remember that His faithfulness is not limited to what has already happened. Trust in His promises for the future. Know that He is faithful to His Word and will continue to guide, provide, and be present in your life. Lastly, remember that reflecting on God's faithfulness is not a one-time activity but an ongoing practice. Nurture your relationship with God through prayer, reading Scripture, engaging in community, and seeking His presence daily. The more you seek Him, the more you will continue to experience and reflect on His faithfulness in your life.

Plan of action:

_____
_____
_____
_____

Foster Healthy Habits

Define the specific healthy habits you want to develop. Be clear about what you want to achieve and why it is important to you. Set realistic and achievable goals that are measurable and time-bound. Focus on one or two habits at a time rather than trying to change everything at once. Starting with small, manageable steps allows you to build momentum and increases the likelihood of success. Once a habit becomes ingrained, you can gradually add new ones. Identify the underlying motivations and reasons behind your desire to develop healthy habits. Whether it's improving your physical health, increasing energy levels, reducing stress, or enhancing your overall well-being, connecting with your motivation can help sustain your commitment. Developing healthy habits requires self-discipline and the ability to overcome challenges. Be prepared for setbacks and occasional lapses. When faced with obstacles, practice self-compassion, learn from setbacks, and recommit to your goals. Cultivate resilience and keep moving forward. Learn about the habits you want to develop. Educate yourself on the benefits, strategies, and best practices related to the specific habits you are cultivating. Seek reliable sources of information, read books, listen to podcasts, or consult professionals who can provide guidance and insights. Acknowledge and celebrate your achievements along the way. Reward yourself for reaching milestones and staying committed to your healthy habits.

Plan of action:

_____
_____
_____
_____

Become a Christian Mentor

Prioritize your own spiritual growth and deepen your relationship with God. Invest time in studying the Bible, engaging in prayer, participating in worship services, and seeking opportunities for personal growth. The stronger your foundation in the Christian faith, the better equipped you'll be to guide and mentor others. Engage with experienced mentors or leaders within your church community. Seek their guidance and wisdom in your own journey as you aspire to become a mentor. They can provide mentorship to you and offer insights into effective mentoring strategies. Additionally, consider attending workshops, seminars, or training programs focused on mentorship within a Christian context. Effective mentoring involves active listening and clear communication. Practice active listening skills, being fully present and attentive to the person you are mentoring. Develop the ability to ask thoughtful questions and provide guidance and feedback in a loving and compassionate manner. Set healthy boundaries with the individuals you mentor to ensure a balanced and productive relationship. Clarify expectations, time commitments, and the scope of your mentorship role. Boundaries help maintain a healthy dynamic and prevent potential issues. Share your own experiences, struggles, and victories with the individuals you mentor. By being vulnerable and authentic, you create a safe space for open dialogue and foster trust. Showing humility and transparency can inspire others and help them navigate their own challenges.

Plan of action:

_____
_____
_____
_____

Attend Christian Counseling

Participate in therapy or counseling sessions that integrate Christian principles, providing additional support and guidance. Recognize that seeking counseling is a positive step towards personal growth, healing, and seeking support. Understand that it is okay to ask for help and that counseling can provide you with tools and resources to address specific challenges or concerns. Look for a Christian counselor who aligns with your beliefs and values. Seek recommendations from trusted individuals, such as pastors, church leaders, or friends who have had positive experiences with Christian counselors. Online directories, professional associations, or referrals from your church community can also be helpful resources in finding Christian counselors. Contact the counselor's office and request an initial consultation appointment. This session will allow you to meet the counselor, discuss your concerns, ask questions, and determine if there is a good fit between you and the counselor. Use this opportunity to assess their approach, level of empathy, and their ability to integrate Christian faith into the counseling process. Once you have chosen a counselor, actively participate in the counseling process. Be open to sharing your thoughts, feelings, and experiences. Engage in the recommended exercises, reflections, or homework assignments provided by the counselor. Remember that counseling is a collaborative effort, and your active involvement contributes to the effectiveness of the process.

Plan of action:

_____
_____
_____
_____

Celebrate Spiritual Milestones

Recognize and celebrate the spiritual growth you experience throughout your recovery journey, acknowledging the transformative work of Christ in your life. Take time to reflect on the significance of the milestone you've reached. Consider how it has impacted your spiritual growth, your relationship with God, and your understanding of your faith. Reflect on the challenges you've overcome and the lessons you've learned along the way. Share your spiritual milestone with trusted friends, family, or members of your faith community. Share your experiences, lessons learned, and insights gained from your journey. Sharing your milestones can inspire and encourage others in their own faith journeys. Consider organizing a special gathering to celebrate your spiritual milestone. Invite close friends, family, or members of your faith community to join you in this celebration. It could be a small intimate gathering, a meal together, or a larger event depending on your preference. Create a keepsake or symbolic item that represents your spiritual milestone. It could be a journal, artwork, a piece of jewelry, or any item that holds personal significance for you. This tangible reminder can serve as a symbol of the milestone and the growth you have experienced. Take the time to document your spiritual milestone and your journey leading up to it. Write about your experiences, challenges, and victories. Capture your thoughts, emotions, and lessons learned. Journaling allows you to reflect on your growth and provides a record of your spiritual journey for future reference.

Plan of action:

_____
_____
_____
_____

Find Strength In Community Worship

Regularly participate in corporate worship, allowing the collective praise and adoration to uplift your spirit and draw you closer to God. Finding strength in community worship can be a meaningful and enriching experience. Actively participate in community worship by attending regular services or gatherings. Get involved in various activities and events they organize, such as group discussions, study circles, volunteer work, or social gatherings. By engaging actively, you'll have more opportunities to connect with others and build meaningful relationships. Reach out to fellow community members, introduce yourself, and initiate conversations. Building relationships within the community can provide a sense of support, encouragement, and shared values. Attend community events or social gatherings to interact with others in a relaxed setting. If you're looking to deepen your spiritual journey within the community, consider seeking guidance from trusted mentors, spiritual leaders, or experienced practitioners. They can provide insights, answer questions, and offer support along your path. Communities often comprise individuals with diverse backgrounds, beliefs, and experiences. Embrace this diversity and strive to learn from others' perspectives. By appreciating different viewpoints, you can broaden your understanding, challenge your assumptions, and foster a more inclusive and supportive community.

Plan of action:

_____
_____
_____
_____

Remain Teachable

Stay open to learning, seeking wisdom from others, and being receptive to constructive feedback, knowing that growth is a lifelong process. Approach new ideas, experiences, and perspectives with an open and receptive mindset. Be willing to consider alternative viewpoints and challenge your own assumptions. Recognize that learning can come from unexpected sources and be open to new possibilities. Cultivate a sense of curiosity and a genuine desire to learn. Ask questions, seek knowledge, and actively engage in learning opportunities. Approach each situation with a beginner's mindset, ready to explore and discover. Develop strong listening skills by giving your full attention when others are speaking. Listen not just to respond but to truly understand. Maintain an open and non-judgmental attitude, and be willing to hear and consider different perspectives and feedback. Recognize that no matter how much you know or achieve, there is always more to learn. Embrace a humble attitude that acknowledges your limitations and the vastness of knowledge and wisdom that exists. Being humble allows you to approach learning with an open mind and a willingness to accept that you don't have all the answers. Instead of fearing or avoiding failure, see it as an opportunity for growth and learning. Embrace a growth mindset that sees setbacks as stepping stones toward improvement. Analyze your failures, identify lessons learned, and apply those insights to future endeavors. Remain open to change and adapt to new circumstances.

Plan of action:

_____
_____
_____
_____

Embrace the Power of Intercessory Prayer

Invite trusted individuals to pray for you and with you, recognizing the strength that comes from collective prayer. Intercessory prayer is a form of prayer where you pray on behalf of others, seeking God's guidance, healing, comfort, or blessings for them. It involves selflessly lifting up the needs, concerns, and well-being of others in prayer. Cultivate empathy and compassion for others. Develop a genuine concern for their well-being and a desire to help. Recognize that intercessory prayer is an act of selflessness, as you are focusing on the needs of others rather than your own. When engaging in intercessory prayer, be intentional and specific about the needs of others. Clearly articulate the concerns, challenges, or desires you are lifting up in prayer. Approach intercessory prayer with faith and trust in the divine's power and goodness. Believe that your prayers can make a difference and that divine intervention is possible. Maintain an attitude of trust, knowing that ultimately the outcome is in the hands of a higher power. When praying for others, especially in personal or sensitive matters, it's important to seek permission and respect confidentiality. Ask for consent and ensure that you honor any requests for confidentiality. Understand that the divine operates in its own timing, which may not always align with our expectations or desires. Be patient and trust that the divine knows what is best for each individual. Embrace a sense of surrender and acceptance, knowing that the divine's plans may be different from our own.

Plan of action:

_____
_____
_____
_____

Share Your Story publicly

Sharing your recovery story publicly can be a courageous and empowering step that has the potential to inspire and support others who may be going through similar experiences. Take time to reflect on your recovery journey. Consider the challenges you faced, the lessons you learned, and the growth you experienced. Reflecting on your story will help you identify key themes, insights, and messages that you want to convey. Before sharing your story, clarify your intentions and purpose. Ask yourself why you want to share your recovery journey publicly. Are you seeking to inspire others, raise awareness, combat stigma, or provide support? Understanding your intentions will help you stay focused and authentic in your storytelling. Authenticity and vulnerability are key in sharing your recovery story. People connect with genuine experiences, struggles, and triumphs. Be honest about your journey, including the challenges you faced, the setbacks you encountered, and the lessons you learned. Share from a place of sincerity and openness. If sharing your recovery story brings up intense emotions or triggers, consider seeking support from a therapist or counselor. Remember that everyone's recovery journey is unique. Respect that others may have different perspectives, experiences, and paths to recovery. Avoid generalizations or prescribing specific solutions. Instead, focus on sharing your story and providing hope, inspiration, and support to those who can relate to your journey.

Plan of action:

_____
_____
_____
_____

Trust In God's Plan

Surrender your recovery journey to God, trusting that He has a purpose for your life and will guide you every step of the way. Cultivate a personal relationship with the divine through prayer, meditation, or other spiritual practices that resonate with you. Engage in regular communication and connection with God to deepen your trust in His presence and guidance. Surrender the need for total control and recognize that there are limits to your understanding and perspective. Trust that God has a broader view and is guiding you in ways that may not always align with your immediate desires or plans. Embrace a sense of surrender and open yourself to the possibilities that God's plan may bring. Trusting in God's plan often requires patience, as His timing may not align with our own expectations. Embrace patience as a virtue and allow things to unfold in their own time. Be open to the lessons and growth that come from waiting and trust that God's timing is perfect. When faced with challenges or difficult circumstances, strive to see them as opportunities for growth and learning. Trust that God allows challenges for a purpose and that they can shape you into a stronger, wiser, and more compassionate person. Look for the lessons and silver linings within the challenges you encounter. During times of uncertainty, challenge, or doubt, lean on your faith and trust in God's plan. Pray for guidance, seek solace in your spiritual practices, and find comfort in the belief that God is with you, even in the midst of hardships. Allow your faith to be a source of strength and resilience.

Plan of action:

_____
_____
_____
_____

Lift Others Up In Prayer

Lifting others up in prayer is a wonderful way to support and show care for those around you. Take a moment to think about the individuals you want to lift up in prayer. Consider their needs, challenges, and desires. Reflect on what specific support or blessings you would like to ask for on their behalf. Clearly articulate your intentions for the person in need. Ask for specific blessings, such as healing, comfort, guidance, strength, or any other areas that are important to them. Be as specific as possible, while also trusting that a higher power will understand and respond accordingly. Ask for general well-being and happiness for the person you are praying for. Pray for their physical, emotional, and spiritual health. You can also pray for their relationships, career, personal growth, and any other areas that you feel are significant. Conclude your prayer by surrendering the outcomes to a higher power. Recognize that you are offering these prayers with trust and faith, and that the ultimate decision lies with a divine force. Let go of any attachments to specific outcomes and allow for divine wisdom to guide the situation. Include prayers that the person you are praying for receives the support, love, and encouragement they need during challenging times. Ask for their burdens to be eased and for them to find solace, wisdom, and strength in difficult circumstances.

Plan of action:

_____
_____
_____
_____

Find Inspiration in Christ

Cultivating a deep relationship with Him and seeking guidance from His teachings and example. Dive into the words of Jesus Christ as recorded in the Bible, particularly the New Testament. Read and reflect on His teachings, parables, and interactions with people. The Gospels of Matthew, Mark, Luke, and John provide valuable insights into His life and ministry. Jesus Christ lived a life of love, compassion, forgiveness, and service. Study His actions and strive to emulate His qualities in your own life. Look for opportunities to show kindness, generosity, and empathy to others. By imitating Christ's example, you can inspire and uplift those around you. Contemplate the sacrificial love of Jesus Christ, who willingly gave His life for the salvation of humanity. Ponder the depth of His love and the significance of His sacrifice. Recognize the power of His grace and forgiveness in your own life, and allow His love to inspire you to love and serve others selflessly. Invite the Holy Spirit, the spiritual presence of Christ, into your life. Ask for guidance, wisdom, and inspiration in your daily endeavors. Trust in the Holy Spirit's ability to guide and empower you to live according to Christ's teachings. Explore Christian literature, including books, devotionals, and biographies that delve into the life and teachings of Christ. Additionally, engage with Christian art, music, and poetry that celebrate His message and inspire devotion.

Plan of action:

_____
_____
_____
_____

Conclusion

Recovering from alcohol and drug addiction through Christ is a transformative journey that requires faith, perseverance, and a commitment to spiritual growth. By incorporating these 100 steps into your recovery process, you can find healing, restoration, and a deeper connection with God. Remember, you are not alone in this journey, and with God's grace, the support of your Christian community, and professional guidance, you can overcome addiction and embrace a life of freedom, purpose, and joy.

About the Author

Throughout his early adulthood, Ryan Sargent struggled with addiction, which led to a series of job changes as he searched for solace and purpose. However, his life took a significant turn when he recognized the need for change and decided to confront his demons head-on. Motivated by his own experiences and a deep desire to help others, Ryan embarked on a path of recovery and personal development. He dedicated himself to understanding the complexities of mental illness and substance abuse, eventually finding employment as a behavioral health technician. For the past decade, Ryan has worked tirelessly with individuals grappling with mental health issues and substance abuse disorders, providing compassion, guidance, and support. Ryan's journey toward healing and self-discovery reached a pivotal moment in October 2021 when he made the life-changing decision to embrace his faith. Through baptism, he found solace, forgiveness, and a renewed sense of purpose. This transformative experience propelled him to share his story and the profound impact of faith with a broader audience. In 2023, Ryan took his passion for inspiring others to the digital realm by starting his own YouTube podcast called "God's Purpose for Your Life." Through this platform, he aims to uplift and encourage individuals from all walks of life, sharing stories of resilience, faith, and the pursuit of meaning. Today, Ryan stands as a living testament to the transformative power of faith, resilience, and self-discovery. With his background as a behavioral health technician, combined with his personal experiences, he offers a rare blend of empathy, understanding, and insight. As a business owner, motivational speaker, podcast host, and author, Ryan Sargent continues to inspire countless individuals on their own journeys of healing, redemption, and self-actualization.